MILLION DOLLAR BEACH HOUSE

My Journey to an EXTRAordinary Life

Cedrick LaFleur

Copyright © 2023 by LaFleur Leadership Books

All rights reserved. No part of this publication may be reproduced, distributed, or transmitted in any form or by any means, including photocopying, recording, or other electronic or mechanical methods, without the prior written permission of the publisher, except in brief quotations embodied in critical reviews and certain other noncommercial uses allowed by copyright law. Printed in the United States of America.

Permission requests should be submitted in writing at one of the addresses below:

Cedricklafleur2@gmail.com
www.lafleurleadershipbooks.com

Paperback ISBN: 979-8-9873658-3-0
Hardback ISBN : 979-8-9873658-4-7

Publisher: Trendy Elite Media Group

This book is intended to provide personal growth and leadership strategies that will assist the reader in their journey to developing the strong leadership and interpersonal skills needed to feel confident and lead fearlessly inside and outside of the workplace. This book is not intended to provide financial, emotional health, or legal advice. Please seek appropriate counsel for financial, emotional health, or legal matters.

TABLE OF CONTENTS

Preface ix

Chapter One: EXTRAordinary Goal Setting:
The Early Years 1

Chapter Two: EXTRAordinary Motivation 13

Chapter Three: EXTRAordinary Father: Men ONLY...........25

Chapter Four: EXTRAordinary Winning with Money.........37

Chapter Five: EXTRAordinary Time Management 57

Chapter Six: EXTRAordinary Leadership 73

Chapter Seven: EXTRAordinary People 85

Chapter Eight: EXTRAordinary Kids 97

Chapter Nine: EXTRAordinary Career..............................115

Chapter Ten: EXTRAordinary Beach House.....................139

Author Bio 155

Success is steady progress toward one's personal goals.
Jim Rohn

DEDICATION

This book is dedicated to my mother, Priscilla Washington, aka Peanut, and my grandparents, Frank and Effie Washington. The lessons I learned from these three people shaped my life today.

My mom didn't play. She was intense, and when she said something, you had better listen because you knew what was coming next. She would talk to you while she was whipping you. As a child, my mom often told me how much she believed in me. She told me, she had high expectations for me and reinforced her love for me. I really miss that.

My grandparents were the salt of the earth. My grandmother spoiled me while my grandfather taught me. Mama Effie, is the one person I wish I could talk to today. She was so kind, gentle and loving. Whatever I wanted to eat, she was cooking it. We spent so much time together.

What keeps me going is my goals.
Muhammad Ali

SPECIAL DEDICATION

My adult journey would not be where it is without Tammie. She has been by my side from day one. Every person needs someone who is willing to run with you, dream with you, fail with them and succeed with them. Our journey has been filled with ups and downs like most relationships, but I wouldn't want to go through it with anyone else. You will not find a detailed chapter about us in this book, because she would not let me give you the TEA. LOL

GET READY TO LAUGH
GET READY TO TEAR UP
GET READY FOR SOME TEA

PREFACE

Everyone has dreams and goals. Achieving personal and professional goals, however, requires planning and action. Learning to manage time and set realistic goals will increase your chance of success in every area of your life. Following the advice in this book will help increase your productivity and help you achieve your dreams.

The stories I'm about to share with you are about my life. The stories I include are my account of what happened at the moment. I include my failures, triumphs, heartbreaks, and setbacks. Take all of them into consideration as you read this book. Failure by itself can hurt if you don't have a winning mindset. All along my journey, failure was close at hand; however, I did not quit.

My life is far from perfect. However, it has been an incredible journey, and much more is to come. I'm a believer that when life hands you lemons, make lemonade. Even during difficult times, I never lost hope. I never stopped believing I would succeed. I never once stopped taking action to get to my next level.

I live by the following six power stories plus the bonus. I hope you read them, put them in your life's mantra, and embrace the lessons in this book. THEY WORK…. Let me repeat it, THEY WORK.

The 6 Power Stories of Life

- Once, all villagers decided to pray for rain. On the day of prayer, all the people gathered, but only one boy came with an umbrella. **That is Faith.**
- When you throw babies in the air, they laugh because they know you will catch them. **That is trust.**
- Every night we go to bed with no assurance of being alive the following day, but still, we set alarms to wake up. **That is Hope.**
- We planned big things for tomorrow despite zero knowledge of the future. **That is confidence.**
- We see the world suffering, but still, we get married and have children. **That is love.**
- A sentence was written on an old man's shirt: "I am not 80 years old; I am sweet 16 with 64 years of experience." **That is attitude.**
- **BONUS:** When anyone asks me how I am doing, I will 100% of the time say, **"I'm always great." That is mindset**

Have a happy day, and live your life like these six stories. Remember: good friends are the rare jewels of life, difficult to find and impossible to replace!!

PREFACE

I have weaved my story with leadership lessons that are important to be ultra-successful. I'm not talking about moderate success. I'm not talking about just making it. I'm talking about the millionaire type of success. People with goals succeed because they know where they are going.

Earl Nightingale

Million Dollar Beach House

Chapter 1

EXTRAordinary Goal Setting: My Early Years

Feb 23, 1967, is the day I was born. That was probably the first day I set goals. As far back as I can remember, I have been a goal-setter. I'm not sure how I learned to set goals, but I always have. I can remember writing goals down for how many friends I wanted to have. In elementary school, I was intentional (I didn't realize that is what it was called) about making friends with certain people. I didn't want to be popular, but I wanted to have specific people as friends.

I also remember setting goals for what items I wanted to buy. Whenever I went to a store with my mom, I would identify the things I wanted to buy at some future date. Then I would write down the item and dream about what I would do when I had that item. My first major purchase with my own money was a cassette recorder from Woolworths for $43. I had to buy it on layaway. Every couple of weeks, I would pay $5 toward the purchase. This store was in downtown Lake Charles on Ryan St. Each time I would go into the store, I would go to the shelf the cassette recorders were on and imagine I owned it already, and I would imagine putting my cassettes in it. I used to press the buttons on the box like I was operating it. I had a date when I knew it would be mine. I did whatever it took to make money to pay it off by that date.

You need goals to get things done. However, not every goal is practical. How you word your goals will determine whether you reach them. When establishing goals, it is essential to remember that they need to be **positive, personal, possible,** and **prioritized**.

They Need to Be Positive

My mother and grandparents always taught me to be positive in every situation. My grandfather used to say, "Being positive will kill all negative people." I used this same philosophy when setting goals. When I was ~5 years old, I lived with my mother in Johnson Hall apartments. There were a lot of kids out there, and we would play outside all day. I preferred to stay outside and play vs. being in the house. My mother had a boyfriend who was mean and evil. I dreamed of leaving that place one day and returning to get my mother out. That was my way of staying positive by staying outside and dreaming.

Whenever we did something he didn't like, he would lock my little brother and me in a closet. Imagine a five-year-old kid being locked in a dark closet for hours. It still upsets me as I write this. I would sit in the closet, scared and nervous. We could not make any noise, or he would get upset. I don't remember him hitting us, but being locked in a closet was like being tortured. After a while in the closet, I dreamed I could fly out of the closet and out of the apartment. I would dream of being with Mama Effie and Pop, my grandparents. That was my safe place.

Whenever I went to their house at 910 N. Blake St., I would beg them to let me stay with them like my older sister. I would tell them I would be a good kid and would never give them any trouble, thinking that would make them say yes. I would call their house weekly to see if they would let me go live with them. After months of begging, my grandfather finally told my grandmother, "Let's go get that boy before something happens to him."

The top picture, the house with the carport, is 910 N. Blake St. These two properties have been in my family since the early 1900s

When creating goals, remember to make sure they are positive. This means you focus on what you want to achieve rather than what you want to avoid. My goal was to live with my grandparents.

For example, you would write, *"I want to live with my grandparents,"* or *"I will achieve a promotion"* rather than *"I don't want to live with this brutal person,"* or *"I will no longer work at this horrible job."*

They Need to Be Personal

Trust me when I say my goal was personal. I wanted that dream to come true more than a 5-year-old could imagine. I could not imagine putting any child through those traumatic events. When creating goals, they need to reflect your dreams and desires. Goals that are not personal are ineffective. Your goals should be about you and only you. I was highly focused on getting out.

My mom would have us get on our knees and say the "Our Father" prayer every night, but I also had a secret prayer I didn't tell anyone. After we said the "Our Father" prayer and got in bed, I would say, "Please, God, make Mama Effie and Pop come get me, and I promise I will be a good kid." Then I would close my eyes and sleep, hoping that when I woke up, I would be in their house.

After months of praying that prayer and dreaming about it daily, I got the phone call I had been waiting for. I will never forget it. It was Saturday evening, and my mom said, Mama Effie wants to talk with you on the phone. I said hello, and she said, "We are coming to get you tomorrow. You are going to come live with us." That was sweet music to my ears. Here is how my next 24 hours went. **Here is the TEA.**

After jumping for joy, I went to my room to start packing. I grabbed my suitcase and put all of my stuff in it. My mom asked,

"Aren't you going to leave clothes here for when you come to visit?" I said, "I'm never coming to visit." My mom asked, "Are you never coming to visit me?" I said, "Mom, I want you to visit me instead." She looked at me and laughed because she knew I was serious.

It was hard for me to sleep that night because I was so excited. Early Sunday morning, I got up, grabbed my suitcase, and walked outside. Mom asked, "Where are you going?" I replied I'm going to wait for Mama Effie and Pop. She said you know they are not coming until after church." Back then, the church was almost all day, but I didn't care. I sat on the porch the entire day with my suitcase, watching for their car to pull up. I didn't want to miss them. I don't even remember eating breakfast or lunch that day. Once they arrived, I ran to their car to get in, and my grandmother said wait; we will visit with your mom first. I said ok, but I sat in the car. I had no intention of stepping foot in that apartment again. No chance of anyone changing their mind or locking me in another closet. After an hour of them visiting, we left, and I never went back. I loved my mom and hated leaving her back there; however, I had no desire to visit her there. But I don't blame her for all of that.

Making goals personal places the burden of responsibility on you, but it also means that other people don't determine when you reach your goals.

Never lower your target; increase your actions.

Too many people give up or lower their goals. Those are people who are not ready to win BIG. Instead, they should increase their actions to see real BIG results.

Cedrick LaFleur

They Need to Be Possible

When creating goals, you need to make sure that they are possible. When you set impossible goals, you set yourself up for failure and disappointment. Creating possible goals demands that you be honest with yourself. I didn't know 100% of my goal of living with my grandparents was possible, but I felt it was. If my older sister lives with them, I can too. I always believed that if someone else can do it, so can I. My mom told me early on that I could do or be whatever I wanted. She also would say, Cedrick, of all my children, I know you will succeed because you are too stubborn not to. There was no change once my mind was made up, even as a child.

Here are goals I remember writing down as a young child:

1. I will buy with my own money a cassette recorder.
2. I will buy two new neckties from Chess King.
3. I will learn how to play piano.

They Need to Be Prioritized

You must know what is essential to you. When I was little, I didn't think about prioritizing goals; I just had goals. As I got older, I thought through the prioritization of goals. I imagine the most important thing for me was getting out of those Johnson Hall Apartments and away from my mom's mean boyfriend.

I found it easy to focus on my goals because I was always a dreamer of a bigger and better life. I didn't know what that meant then; I knew something else was out there. As a child, I spent much time dreaming about being a wealthy businessman. Those dreams kept me focused on meeting my goals. And once I achieved it, I added another goal. A friend reminded me a few years ago about something I used to say to her when we used to play in Shattuck Street Park. I always told her, "One day, we will be rich and move away from here."

Don't get me wrong; I had a perfect childhood. I loved growing up in North Lake Charles. In Goosport, on Blake St., I loved it. I had a lot of cousins and a lot of friends, and we enjoyed each other. If you grew up on that side of town, you were considered poor, but I didn't consider us poor. None of my friends considered that they were poor. We never went without. Our power never was out; we always had food and new clothes. The people in our neighborhood had pride in their homes and yard. Maybe we had little money, but it didn't show in our attitudes. We knew all our neighbors, and they knew my mother and grandparents, so I would dare to act up. Children respected their parents in our neighborhood. I was a stubborn kid with a deep voice that dreamed a lot. I was a different type of kid; I loved dressing up, debating with you, and thinking about big ideas.

Examples of some things I dreamed about:

1. **Being a wealthy businessman:** I didn't even know what a business was. My idea of a businessman was the dad on the show *Leave It to Beaver*. He wore a black suit, white shirt, black tie, and a briefcase when he walked in from work. So, when I got older, that was how I dressed.

2. **Living in a big fancy house:** I only knew of the houses my grandmother cleaned. Those houses were big, brick, and really nice. When I went with her, I imagined that it was my house with my stuff. I would sit and think about what I would do in my house. I also dreamed about this when my grandfather and I would cut "white people's yards." That's what we called it. Those yards were on the other side of town, far from where I lived. The yards and the houses were prominent, at least to me. Every time I cut the grass

or pulled weeds, I told myself that this type of house would be mine one day. Now I pass by some of those houses and think that house is small.

3. **Having my own Lowrey Teenie Genie organ:** In the Prien Lake Mall, there was a music store that sold musical instruments, and they had this organ with red, green, and yellow buttons. Every time we went to the mall, I would go into the store, sit on the bench, act like that was my organ, and play all kinds of songs. I would never push the buttons because I was afraid I could break them. I would just sit and imagine. Sometimes I would just walk by and look at it. I wanted it so bad.

4. **Having my dad bring McDonald's for lunch for my entire class** never came true, but I would imagine it and imagine how happy I would be if it did. However, I fulfilled this dream differently by doing this for my children's class. I remember the excitement on their faces when I walked into the cafeteria with boxes of Kid's Meals for everyone. They just didn't know I was more excited than they were. I was living my childhood dream.

5. **My friends and cousins came to my birthday party all dressed up (see the picture below):** This never happened, even though I requested it. I used to tell my mom I would be upset if people didn't come to my party dressed up, and guess what? No one would come dressed up. Notice in the picture that I was dressed up. I envisioned a proper party with everyone in nice clothes. I was usually the only one dressed up for my party. I used to think, don't these kids want nice stuff? LOL. But we had a good time anyway.

SIDE NOTE: From 9th grade to 12th grade, I dressed up with a shirt and tie and carried a briefcase daily. I was pretending I was a businessman.

Practical Illustration

Antonio T. was miserable at his job. He knew he needed a change and created life goals to spur change. He created the goal, *"No longer work at this horrible job."* He continued with, *"My family will respect my decisions."* Antonio also created a short-term goal to find a position in upper management even though he had no management experience. Over the year, Antonio tried to realize his goals, but he remained in the same place. Feelings of frustration led him to seek life classes where he learned to create more practical goals. After following the Four Ps, Antonio began to meet his goals.

You remember that time when "they" said **YOU ARE NOT GOOD ENOUGH.**

You remember that time when "they" said **YOU ARE NOT READY**.

I DO.

But I also remember ALL the times I told myself, **I'M GOOD ENOUGH.**

I also remember ALL the times I told myself, **I'M READY**.

I also remember ALL the times I told myself, **I'M GONNA KEEP GOING.**

**GRIT: Never Give up regardless of what "they" say.
Just keep going.**

Cedrick LaFleur

Chapter Two
EXTRAordinary Motivation

Motivation is internal and self-driven. It's not something someone else can give you. It's either you have it or you don't. Goals can inspire, but that inspiration can fade into the reality of everyday life. To meet your goals, you must motivate yourself. You cannot constantly rely on external motivation. Starting different methods of motivation, such as remembering peak moments, writing down goals, and gamification, will help keep you focused and positive as you work towards your goals.

I was always a self-motivated child. I rarely did things that everyone else did just because "they" did. I had my ideas and opinions of what I wanted to do or not do. My older sister went to Oak Park Jr High, so my mom wanted me to transfer from Pearl Watson Jr High, but I did not want to. She did a fantastic thing for me when she let me debate her with reasons I should stay at Pearl Watson. I gave her my reasons, but she still did not agree. We debated back and forth for about 30 minutes. Notice I use the word debate. She knew I needed that versus just telling me what I would do.

I told her all my friends were at Pearl Watson, and if I had to go to Oak Park, I would not make new friends. I would not play in the band or do anything extra. I was motivated not to go to that school. In the end, she decided that I could stay at Pearl Watson. I knew she had just paid $300 for a new trumpet, and she did not want that just to sit. I WAS MOTIVATED.

Remember Peak Moments

Positive memories are potent motivators. Remembering peak moments creates a sense of achievement and encourages us to seek that feeling again. Peak moments are not relegated to work accomplishments. They are any strong memories that create positive feelings. For example, completing a marathon may be a peak moment. Getting married or having a child can also be peak moments. Looking back over your peak moments will show you how much you already have and how far you have come. They will encourage and motivate you to keep moving forward and reach your goals.

I have had many peak moments in my short life. However, I want you to know if you think about it, you also have had many peak moments. I will share several of my peak moments and want you to consider yours. At the end of this section, I encourage you to take a break and write down your peak moments. This will excite you, motivate you, and encourage you to keep going when the subsequent adversity strikes.

A Few of My Peak Moments:

The day my mom surprised me with my trumpet in 7th grade was a Peak Moment. By now, she was living in a family house next door to my grandparents. She came home from work and asked me to go to her car to get something out of the trunk. Like most kids, I was thinking, why didn't she just get it out of the trunk when she got out of the car? However, back then, I would not say that out loud. It was only a thought in my mind. So, I opened the trunk, thinking I was looking for something for her. I saw this trumpet case in the trunk, and my facial expression changed immediately. It went from frown to joy in a heartbeat. I protected that trumpet with all my might. I still have it. I knew how much that cost her, so I wanted to protect it.

Another peak moment was when I found out I would go to Washington Marion High School for my senior year. I was one of those students who went to four schools in high school. Not because we moved or anything because we lived in the same house. The school district was going through a transition. My 9th-grade year was at Pearl Watson Jr High; in 10th grade, I went to Lake Charles High School. Then my junior year schools merged, so I was at Lake Charles-Boston High School. Then my senior year, I was scheduled to go to Washington Marion. The band director at WM, Henry "Huck" Thomas, talked to me at the end of my junior year to tell me he was losing many trumpet players and hoped I would transfer there.

At first, my mother opposed it only because she was a graduate of W.O. Boston, and she wanted one of her children to be associated with her school. I wanted to go to WM, so the "debate" started. I will never forget this conversation. She told me all her reasons for me to stay at LCB, but I was not focused on any of that. I wanted to be in the WM band, which was the city's most prominent and best band. People would come from all over the watch their band perform. As a good trumpet player, I wanted to be a part of the best. My sole reason was the band. I would counter her agreement with, their band is the best.

For about 2 hours, we discussed this in my grandmother's den. Finally, she caved and said well, you can't go until the beginning of next school year, which would be my senior year. That was a significant victory for me because anyone who knows my mother knows she could debate with the best of them. I told people the next day I was leaving and going to WM to be in the band. The band director at LCB, Mr. Beaco, met with me and tried to rationalize why I should stay at LCB. Like most teens, I listened, but I thought this was a waste of time because I would play in that band. I WAS MOTIVATED.

During that summer, I practiced every day. I went to McNeese's summer band camp to be ready to play in that band. When motivated, you will move mountains to reach your goal.

Write Down Your Goals

Knowing your goals is not enough to motivate you; you must write them down. Writing down goals creates a visual reminder of where you are going. When writing down your goals, remember to:

Use the present tense: This will help you visualize reaching your goals.

Use "I" statements: An "I" statement reinforces that they are personal goals. They are your responsibility.

Example:

I will go to Washington Marion HS.

I will be a wealthy businessman.

Once your goals are written, display them someplace where you will see them regularly. Not only do I write my goals on my phone, but I also set a reminder so I can say them every day. Not some days. Not most days. Not every other day, but every day.

At 19 years old, I got married. I must admit that was not one of my goals. I had never thought about getting married. During my dreams of being a wealthy businessman in a big fancy house, I never thought about being married. I dreamt of having kids, but the married part didn't come to my mind. All of that changed in one day. **Here is the TEA.**

I was in my freshman year at McNeese State University and was asked to take the lead role in a play called "A Wedding Band." Mr. Blanchard, a teacher at WM high school, was leading this play which needed a trumpet player as the lead role. I was honored he asked, but I was nervous because I had never been in a high-level production like this. My character's name was Blaze Thornton, the handsome trumpet player. That was me in real life. I'm just saying. But I was not going to say no. So I showed up at the first rehearsal, and the person playing my girlfriend in the play was Tammie Johnson; her character was Deanna. I didn't know her, but I wanted to get to know her once I saw her.

In this play, there was also this girl whose character was Lasha. In the play, Lasha and I were best friends growing up, and she secretly had a crush on me. I just saw her as a good friend. The script in the play was that she would tell me she had a crush on me once she found out I was getting married.

While practicing for this play, Tammie and I started to like each other in real life. One day we had a conversation and started dating. The drama started when I had to break up with my then-current girlfriend to start dating Tammie. I said earlier that life happens. On that day, it did. That was not my plan. However, it happened. Our relationship was different. I won't go into the drama of her wearing my class ring to school the next day and my ex finding out. Let me move on.

We had great chemistry practicing for the play, and that chemistry sparked well outside of the play. I suppose you are picking up what I'm putting down. One day we had to promote a short skit for the play at the local TV station (KPLC). She and "Lasha" rode with me to the TV station, then, on the way home, they were arguing over whom I was dropping off first. Well, I dropped Lasha off first, then Tammie and I took the long route to her house. I was the good-looking college guy, and she was in high school, girl. It was nothing major we just made out. I put a hickey on her neck, and the next day, her mom called me, and she was hotter than fish grease. I was respectful on the phone but was a typical 19-year-old boy once I hung up. I said, woman, please, go sit down with all that.

Fast forward a few months into the relationship, and she discovers she is pregnant. Then everything got serious. I got another phone call from her momma. She said, "Do you know that my daughter is pregnant?" I wanted to say, "And," but I said, "Yes, ma'am." Then she said, "You have two choices, either you all get married, or she will have an abortion." Once she finished, I replied, "No girlfriend of mine is having an abortion. So you might as well start planning a wedding." Then she handed the phone to Tammie. I asked, "Did you hear the conversation?" She replied, "Yes." So I said, "Well, we are getting married." She said, "Okay," and we hung up.

So now we have been married for 36 years, and I still have not proposed. That would have been the romantic thing to do, but it did not happen that way for us. So not all goals will be written, and life circumstances will happen. Sometimes you must be willing to move at the moment with responsibility and accountability.

I could have run away from this and said, that's her problem and not mine, but that would not have been right. That would not have been me.

Was I ready to get married? Probably not.

Was I financially sound to handle all of that? Definitely Not.

Was I mature enough to understand everything I was signing up for? Nope

Was I ready to be accountable for my actions? YES

Was it hard? YES

Did we have naysayers? YES

Did we listen to them? NO

Your decisions in difficult moments will define your life, so you must be ready to handle them when they come. You can't put your obligation on someone else. You must stand up and stand tall in the face of adversity.

We didn't have much in the first few years, and there were people who tried to break us up. But we were steadfast. I remember receiving a nasty card in the mail; someone was trying to create doubt. I read it, looked at Tammie, and said, we will be okay. I'm going to be here, and we will do some great things together. I threw the card out and kept it moving. You must know your goal and let no one or nothing sidetrack you.

GOD believes in you, so it's time to believe in yourself and God's plan for your life and future (Jeremiah 29:11)!

Track Your Progress

Finally, tracking your progress will help you see your accomplishments and which areas require more effort. I will share with you how I tracked my goals. Additionally, seeing your improvements will motivate you to continue your hard work. Over time, you should see yourself consistently reaching more of your daily goals. There are different ways to track progress.

I track some of my goals in my Notes app on my iPhone. For my financial goals, I usually use an Excel spreadsheet. I will talk specifically about my personal financial goals in another chapter. However, I want you to understand that a clear picture of your finances is a significant part of your success. If you think you can do it "willy nilly," I'm telling you, you will fail.

The Law of Navigation states, "Anyone can steer a ship, but it takes a leader to chart the course."

The Story: Roald Amundsen and Robert F. Scott set out to be the first to reach the South Pole. Amundsen planned well, and Scott did not, resulting in the death of him and his entire team.

The Lesson: Amundsen understood what was needed to "navigate" successfully to the South Pole. He had the right plan with the right people.

You may do it by hand, using a spreadsheet, or using an online tool. Despite your format, charting requires you to complete a list of daily goals. At the end of each day, you check off the goals that you accomplished. Do not expect always to reach all of your goals. Tracking progress shows you the areas that need more of your focus.

Stop reading right now and write down some of your Peak Moments. Seriously, I want you to do it NOW. If you put it off, you will never do it.

1. _____
   _____
   _____
2. _____
   _____
   _____
3. _____
   _____
   _____

Practical Illustration

Whitney C. was having trouble staying motivated. She looked at her goals every day. They were written in the present tense and used I statements, but she lost focus by the end of the day and had too many unfinished tasks. One day, her mentor told her about the gamification program the company would implement. She thought gamification would be effective for her personal goals since she loved playing games in her spare time. Whitney created her own game with the tasks she hated, such as exercising. After three months, Whitney discovered she was reaching more of her goals. Gamification made her task quests to be conquered, and she found herself excited to finish and earn better rewards.

BONUS

I want to give you a better since of the change I wanted to make for my family. Growing up as a poor, black person in America was not a curse nor a burden. However, I wanted more for my life and my children. I wanted generational change for my family.

My mom had a baby as a teenager. Tammie's mom had a baby as a teenager. I wanted different for my children. Neither of us were born into financial wealth. Yes, we had family wealth, meaning the love from our family. But I wanted more than that. I wanted to give my kids resources for a better life.

To do this, we could learn lessons from the Jewish community. One book I learned from was "Thou Shall Prosper," by Rabbi Daniel Lapin. Here is an excerpt.

2% of US population is Jewish. However they make up 40% of the wealthiest people in America. Based on stats there should only be about 8 Jews on Forbes 400 list, however in reality there are between 60-100 on the list. Jewish households with income of greater than $75,000 is double that of non-Jews.

Why is that? Because they have a disproportionally high literacy rate and a respect for education. They deny themselves temporary pleasures for long-term good.

Lesson:

1. The more wealth people accumulate around me, the more I will accumulate.
2. If you are not interested in making money, then this book will not be for you.
3. Is gaining wisdom all about increasing wealth? No. The reverse is true, gaining wealth is all about increasing

wisdom and improving your ability to get along with others.
4. Jewish tradition teaches after you have done new things for a while, you will feel yourself becoming a new person. (Ex: think about how you feel when you started exercising vs. how you feel after a few months of it).
5. Success requires learning and practice. When you grow, you become a new person. (Think about being baptized, it means you should become a new person).
6. How do you become a better negotiator?
   a. **Learn.** Learn the technique
   b. **Understand.** Understand those principles behind the technique. How they work provides assurance they will work.
   c. **Practice.** Practicing to become proficient and to become a different person. Like becoming a "practicing Christian," the implication means by consistently practicing religiously mandated behaviors, by doing different things, I will integrate the desired habits into myself, eventually becoming a new person.

Law of Fatherly Navigation:

Any man can steer a ship, but it takes a father to chart the course.

In other words, any man can become a father, but it takes a real man to become a daddy.

Chapter Three

EXTRAordinary Fathers: Men ONLY

I'm writing this chapter for men. Let me rephrase that; I'm writing this chapter for those EXTRAordinary fathers.

> *"Anyone who tells you fatherhood is the greatest thing that can happen to you, they are understanding it."*
>
> — Mike Myers

From the day I learned that I would be a father, I knew exactly what I would do and not do as a father. I knew the father I wish I had as a kid. I knew what I wanted my father to do and be, but that never happened. So that clarified my vision of what type of father I would be.

In my early teenage years, I decided to be a father in my kid's life. I wanted to be the type of father whose kids shared experiences with. I wanted to be the type of father whose kids wanted to talk, laugh, and cry with. Remember, in an earlier chapter, I said I dreamed of my father buying kids' meals for my entire class. I was committed to doing that for my children.

I wanted to be known as a great dad.

This would be the first grandchild for my mother and Tammie's parents. We got married before the baby was born and were nervous and excited. One day we thought about what we would name the baby. So we went out and bought a baby names book, remember this was before the internet days. We had a list of both girls' and boys' names. I was convinced we would have a baby boy. In addition, all the old wives' tales about how to tell what she was having also claimed she was having a boy. So, we were all set to have a baby boy. We also did all the usual baby preparation things, like keeping a bag packed and birthing classes.

I remember early one morning, around 1 am, Tammie woke up with contractions. I jumped up and woke her little brother who was at our house. We all jumped in my old 1971 Ford Pinto with slick tires and headed to the hospital. That evening it had been raining so the roads were wet. As we rushed to the hospital, we approached the intersection of Enterprise Blvd and Broad St; the light changed to yellow, then red, so I slammed on the brakes. At that moment, I realized that was the wrong thing to do. Slick tires and wet roadways at a high rate of speed do not work well together. That car started spinning faster than a snowball rolling downhill. When we finally stopped spinning, we were headed in the opposite direction. I turned and looked in the back seat at Tammie's little brother; his eyes were bigger than two-quarters. I laughed and asked him if he was okay. Poor thing, he just shook his head yes. We eventually started heading to the hospital at a much slower speed. When we got to the hospital, they put her in a triage room, and after several hours, they released her and said it was a false alarm.

We had several false alarms during this pregnancy. Then one afternoon on April 15, I received a phone call at work, letting me know that Tammie was at the hospital getting ready to have the baby. I left work and arrived at the hospital a little nervous about my baby boy's appearance. I was thinking about all the boy names we had selected and couldn't wait to see him. Back then, you could not go into the delivery room. After a while, the elevator door opened, and the nurse came down to look for me. She said congratulations, you have a new baby girl. I said what, a girl? Are you sure? She said yes. Then she asked, "Are you ready to go see her?" I said yes.

We got in the elevator, made it to the floor, and I walked over to the viewing window, and the nurse pointed her out. All I saw at first were these little, long feet. I thought, wow, she has long feet. But I was happy to have my little, long feet daughter. I went into the room to see Tammie, and she was okay. The name we had decided on was TreKessa Lorraine. I don't remember anything else at the hospital. All I remember was that a few days later, they both came home.

This was the first grandchild and let me say it was special. Tammie's parents stepped into being grandparents. I don't remember buying any clothes the first year; it seems as though they were always buying something new for our little TreKessa. I was excited about my baby girl. I was so protective of her and didn't let everybody hold her.

This was the ultimate thrill of life, having this baby girl depending on me for everything. I'm not sure how any father would not cherish this experience. During the first year, Tammie was still in high school, so I greatly cared for the baby. I changed her diapers. I dressed her. I combed her hair with all her little barrettes. I always took my time to make sure she looked good. I remember watching the Oliver North Congressional hearings while combing her hair many mornings. She didn't realize what we were watching, but she and I would enjoy our time together. I cherished every minute of it. I call them **Dad Moments**.

***Dad Moments** are times when you are creating special memories with your child.*

I remember not letting her ride in any car that did not have a car seat (this was in the early stages of requiring car seats; many people still road without them). I remember buying a swimming pool for us to play in. She was too young to realize what was happening, but I enjoyed spending a lot of time with my little girl. I enjoyed lying on the floor and playing with her. These were some of the best times in my life. **Dad Moments.**

A year later, I left to join the U.S. Air Force, and once all my training was over, they came to join me at Shepherd AFB, TX. I was so excited to see my bundle of joy, but she was not so excited to see me. She would not let me hold her or stay alone during her first week there. She was so young she forgot who I was. I was crushed. But after that first week, we were bonded again. I loved my little girl and wanted to spend every moment with her.

Fast forward to 1992; we were living in Florida by then. I was 25, and Tammie was 23 when I discovered we were having another baby. We were both excited to have another child. This time, we would find out the sex of the child. Finally, it was a boy. Although I loved my baby girl, I was super excited to have a son. We had decided on Patrick Jamal as the name. Many people asked if we were going to name him Junior. Absolutely not. That puts too much pressure on a child, and I wanted him to be authentic and create his own identity. Tammie would have a Cesarean, so we settled on August 13. As that date approached, the anticipation ramped up. We were better prepared this time around compared to our first. Finally, it was that day. We made it to the hospital. As we were in the birthing room, I don't know if her water just broke or if it was induced, I remember seeing the indentation of a baby in her stomach. They rushed to get him out, and little Patrick came into our life and this world.

In my mind, our family was complete. I decided I didn't want any more children; I just wanted to be the best husband and daddy to these two children. I was so convinced at age 25 I wanted no more children that I scheduled to have a vasectomy without even talking to Tammie. She was upset, nervous, and shocked once she discovered I was going to do that. I set up a time for her to talk with the surgeon independently, but I had decided. Finally, she agreed, which was the end of that—no more children.

Now that I have set the stage, let me tell you the rest of this story. Let me give you the **TEA**. By the end of this chapter, you will see why I'm talking directly to you. I will share several experiences and my perspective on being an EXTRAordinary father.

Men have an obligation that they should lean into. I see too many men making babies and then making excuses for not caring for them. I also see too many women letting this behavior exist. Men, it is our responsibility to be a father to our children. Even though my father was not in my life, my grandfather, Frank Washington Sr., showed me how a real man does it. One of my uncles, Uncle Paul, modeled what a good father looked like. He doesn't know it, but I was watching him. He is a remarkable and fun uncle. I'll talk about my grandfather more later. As I said earlier, I combed my daughter's hair, dressed them, cooked for them, changed their diapers, and disciplined them. It was my duty, obligation, and responsibility. It was also my pleasure to do it. Because they were my children. **Dad Moment**

One memorable moment I will never forget with my son was Saturday afternoon. The kids were all playing outside in our driveway. We had a big driveway, so all the neighborhood kids would play there. I walked outside through the garage. I looked at them playing, then called and asked him what he was doing. He started telling me, then I asked him, "Do you know that you are special?" His eyes lit up and got real big, and he asked softly, "Am I special?" I said, yes, son, you are special. He smiled and went back to playing. At that moment, I knew I had positively affected him forever. I can only imagine what was going through his mind; I could tell something was. That look on his face is etched in my mind for the rest of my life. Those are the **Dad Moments** I live for.

In June 1996, we were living in Palm Bay, Florida. Abbott Laboratories offered me a job; however, they were moving us to Dallas. Tammie was coming up on her senior year of college and needed to complete a 1-year hospital internship. So, moving was not an ideal thing at this time for her. I wanted her to stay in Florida while I moved to Texas, but she did not want to. So we all moved to Texas. Then one Sunday, it all changed.

We visited a local church with an Abbott colleague and his family; then, we went to lunch at Pappadeaux. After wrapping up lunch and visiting them at their house on the drive home, Tammie made a comment that changed everything. She said, "I will be glad when we get in their position, done with school and living a better life." That was it; I hit the steering wheel and then pulled over on the side of the road. **Here is the TEA.** I turned to her and said, "You are not ready for that yet because you are following me. I said if you were ready for that, then you would have stayed in Florida to complete your internship. We will be separated for 12-14 months; then, it will be over. You go back to Florida, and I will keep the kids with me, and we will be fine."

She asked, "How will you take care of the kids?" I said it's easy; I'm their father, so I will figure it out. I said, you are going to school and don't need to worry about the children. I will work each day and can be home with them. The following week, she returned to Florida to complete her 12-month internship.

THINKING MOMENT:

Would you have made that decision?
Are you prepared to make that type of sacrifice or commitment for your family?

Did I know how I would make it all happen? No, absolutely not. But I knew I would make it work. Because I had dreams, goals, and higher aspirations, and nothing would get in the way. So, now it was our 9-year daughter, our 4-year son, and me in a one-bedroom apartment making it work. We had just gone through bankruptcy before we moved. Now I was paying apartment rent in Texas, a house payment in Florida, and an apartment for Tammie in another city in Florida. We were determined not to get into a financial crisis again, but we needed to make these next 12 months work out. I was only making $38,100 per year. Even in 1996, that was not much money, but it was more than I had made before. Imagine having a college degree, being a nationally certified Medical Laboratory Scientist, and making this salary which was significantly more than I made in the hospital laboratory.

During that year, I did homework with my daughter. I combed her hair and got them ready for school. I found a service called Pea Pod that would let you order groceries, and they would deliver them to our front door. I would play a game with the kids, giving each $1 to put groceries up. But I would add fun by saying, "Let's see who could put up the most items." They each would rush to get items out of the bag and put them on the shelf. I didn't care what shelf the items would be on long as they would be put on the shelf. It was fun for them, and they liked earning money. The benefit was that I didn't have to put up the groceries. **WIN/WIN**. We didn't have a lot of extra funds, so I found a $1 movie theater not far from the house so we would go there every few weekends. I found a local park we would go to, and we played many games inside. **Dad Moments**.

WE DEVELOPED A SYSTEM since I was still at work when they left school, and we didn't have cell phones. They would lock the door and call my office when they got home from school. Then I would call them before I left the office to come home. When they would hear the door open, they would hide in their secret spot until I came in and said, "It's me."

When TreKessa started playing sports, we spent time with basketball, then baseball, then basketball again. I remember signing her up for a baseball team; it was an all-boys team when we arrived. Although the coach let her on the team, you could tell he nor any of the players were happy about it. Then comes the first game, and things change. They set her up to bat last and put her on third base. After each practice, I would tell her to keep working, and she will show them. Finally a game day, she got a chance at bat. Swing, the bat hit the ball and left the park. All those attitudes started to warm up. Then she chased a player down who tried to steal to home plate. That changed things even more. Suddenly, she was now the designated hitter. She learned her value during that experience.

Men, my point in talking about my experience is that I want you to know that you can and should do this as well. Very few men say, "I'll take the kids with me to another state while you stay back and finish school." However, I know there are some EXTRAordinary men out there who are doing it every day. Keep doing it because your children are counting on you.

I get so upset when I hear women say they don't get relief from raising their children or have to rush home because their husband is home with the kids, and they must ensure they are okay. I usually tell them they will be okay; they will do it. And if she stops facilitating that type of mindset, then things will change. There is no such thing as men "babysitting" their kids. We have an obligation and responsibility to care for our kids, so we can do everything that women do to care for our children.

Part of being an EXTRAordinary father is also understanding your weak areas. We all have them, and I understand mine.
I wasn't the father who:

1. Taught my kids how to change the oil in their cars. (Pepboys/Jiffy Lube did all that) LOL
2. Showed them how to cut the grass. (That's why we have a lawn guy)

3. Taught them how to use a hammer and screwdriver. (That's what grandfathers are for)
4. Showed them how to build things. (That's what uncles do)

However, I gave them the resources to do everything. By resources, I don't just mean money. Through resources, I helped them with critical thinking skills, financial literacy, personal growth, and development. In addition, I was responsible for teaching my son what an EXTRAordinary man was and showing my daughter how she should value herself.

As a man, you must be comfortable enough with yourself to allow other people to teach them things. That's what I also mean by resources. I'm very comfortable with who I am and who I'm not. They talked to their uncles and grandfather to learn what I was weak at. That is not my strength zone, so I stayed away from that. You must identify your weak areas and become okay with them. An EXTRAordinary father is a counselor, mentor, coach, guide, and resource whenever and however your kids need you. My kids know my weak areas, and if I tried to pretend that those things were a strength, I would just be fooling myself and not them. My kids respect me more because I operate better in my strength zone. And I'm comfortable with letting others teach them.

Becoming a father is a gift, but becoming a daddy is a choice.

Every situation/relationship brings different dynamics, so don't get upset with my words. I'm not talking about your specific situation but the broader picture of men raising their children and creating **Dad Moments**. We have a fantastic opportunity to be fathers to children:

To ENCOURAGE them,
To MENTOR them,
To COACH them,
To INSPIRE them,

To DEVELOP them,
To INFLUENCE them,
To IMPACT them,
To EMPOWER them.

That is one opportunity you cannot and should not abdicate. This is not about the mother; this is about the children. And they are counting on you.

At the end of those 12 months, Tammie graduated from college and joined us in Texas. Looking back on it, she agreed it was the right decision, and that time passed quickly. Nothing will get in the way when you have your eye on a bigger prize. No one will get in the way when you know what you want.

When we got married, we were committed to never giving up on our goal of both of us graduating from college. I would not let that happen. And by the summer of 1997, we were both college graduates. We were breaking the generational curse.

We were committed to a different and better life for our family, even though we had naysayers.

We were committed to goals more significant than anything we could have in Lake Charles. I know I pushed Tammie to stretch herself and get outside her comfort zone.

Here is the TEA: People told her, "Don't let your husband go to Texas alone because those women will take your husband." I told her, if I'm going to leave you, it won't matter if you are there, so stop listening to bad advice.

"If the plan doesn't work, change the plan, but NEVER change the goal."

Winning with money is 80% behavior 20% head knowledge.

Dave Ramsey

Chapter 4

EXTRAordinary Winning with Money

Undoubtedly, **winning with money** is among the most challenging things for most people. However, as the beginning quote says, winning with money is 80% behavior and 20% head knowledge. That means we must be intentional with every dollar. Remember, I said earlier, I wanted to make a generational change for my family. In this chapter, you will see examples of the generational change we had to make.

My grandfather tried his best to teach me how to win with money. He said things like:

"If you can't pay cash for it, you don't need it."
"Save your money for a rainy day."
"Don't let that money burn a hole in your pocket."
"You don't need a checkbook if you pay cash."

When I grew up, we were considered poor, but I didn't know that then. I didn't realize my grandparents didn't have a lot of money. From my perspective, they had a lot of resources. I guess that is why my grandfather was trying to teach me lessons. Like most children, we don't pay attention to those lessons. Or I didn't listen when I was younger. However, as I got into a financial crisis, those lessons started to resonate with me more and more.

When I was a freshman at McNeese State University, I was on a band scholarship and received I grant. Since my scholarship covered most of my tuition, I would receive the rest of my Pell Grant checks, which was one happy day. I would spend that money as fast as I received it. Like most students, I would go into the finance office every few days to see when I would get that check. That money burned a hole in my pocket even before receiving it. I should have recognized that was the start of my bad spending habits.

Just as success leaves clues, so do your bad habits. You have to be willing to pay attention to the signs. I was not paying attention to the signs or my spending behavior. I will share some behaviors that I recognize in me and how to overcome them. It is essential to understand that you can correct your lousy spending behavior if you are intentional with the steps we provide.

There is no quick fix to winning with money. It is not an overnight process. It is a journey that you must be willing to take.

- Any person can win with money if they are willing to follow the process.
- Any person can win with money if they are willing to change their financial decisions.
- Any person can win with money if they are willing to stop trying to keep up with the Joneses.
- Any person can win with money if they are willing to give up short-term gratification.

The year was 1992; I was 25 years old, and we lived in base housing on Patrick AFB, FL. Life was good; we had no financial issues. The only debt we had was one car payment. Some of my grandfather's financial lessons were creeping into my mind. We started discussing buying a house one day because we saw friends and coworkers in the building process. So we ventured out on Sunday afternoon after church to look at subdivisions. For several weeks, we looked at new home builders after new home builders. There were a lot of new subdivisions going up, and we could see ourselves in any of them.

Then one Saturday afternoon, we found ourselves in Palm Bay talking to a homebuilder and seeing all the beautiful designs. Building a new home in that area was so enticing and affordable. After looking at several floor plans, we decided on the one we liked. It was a four-bedroom, 2 Bathrooms, 2000-square-foot house for only $96,000. I asked the builder; we could build this house for less than $100,000? The builder rep said yes. On that day, we filled out the application for a home loan. I was thinking, this is the American dream, and these two kids from the north side of Lake Charles were coming up.

This is the current day house, but it was pink when we built it.

All week, Tammie and I were thinking about what furniture we would get and how each room would be set up. We were dreaming big time all week. One week later, we were back in front of the builder to see if our application had been approved. We walked in, sat down then he said something that rocked me with his words. He said, "You have some of the best credit and credit scores I have seen for people your age. Your application has been approved." I was proud of what he said. However, that statement caused me so many problems later.

That single statement bolstered my ego and financial mindset. That one statement gave me a sense of success and caused me to overuse my newfound creditworthiness. At the moment, I didn't realize how that statement affected my understanding of financial success. Creditors want you to believe that a high credit score signifies financial success or power. However, the reality is quite the opposite.

Your **FICO SCORE** is:

- 35% **DEBT PAYMENT HISTORY**
- 30% **DEBT OWED**
- 15% **HOW LONG YOU'VE BEEN IN DEBT**
- 10% **NEW DEBT**
- 10% **TYPES OF DEBT**

Your high credit score shows how much debt you have and how well you have managed it. It is another way to keep you in debt. It is not an indicator of your financial health or wealth. Sure, you can borrow more money. However, **that is the trap.** The less you use your credit, the lower your score will be, and at some point, if you don't use credit, you won't have a score.

The rich rule over the poor, and the borrower is a slave to the lender. Proverbs 22:7

I'm not making excuses for my poor spending habits. However, I'm trying to give you the context of what caused me to go down the slippery slope to bad money management.

Fast forward to early 1993; we have not only moved into our new home, but we have a new baby boy. We were living the American dream: A new house, two nice cars, and two little children. We didn't have a dog, a white picket fence, and the money to aff ord it all. The first few years, things were going well; we had no issues. However, we started spending more and more.

Here is the TEA.

It all started so quickly with the words, "It will only cost $10 per month." That simple phrase gives you the mindset that you can afford anything. "Mr./Mrs. LaFleur, we will make it easy for you; this will only cost $20 per month, $15 per month, $12 per month." I'm sure you've experienced this as well. After a while, you realize those small fees are adding up. By mid-1995, I started realizing we had more month left than money. We only had a mortgage and all these "easy small" payments. The problem is, we had so many.

I can appreciate where we are today because I went through this experience. Although it was a challenging and trying time for us, it helped make me a better person today. Have you been through this?

I have always been a person who could figure out how to overcome difficult moments. The way I figured out how to make it through was to use the cars we owned as collateral. Outside military bases were payday loan companies. One day,

I decided to see how it worked. They walked me through the process, and I thought, oh, this will work. It was so easy; I gave them the title to my car, and they gave me the money I needed. Then I would agree to pay it back on payday with interest. I wasn't concerned about the interest, only getting the money I needed to help me make it until payday. Have you ever been in one of those situations where you will do anything to get out of the crisis, so you didn't worry about what you had to do? I was there. But on payday, I would make it there, pay the loan back, and get my title back. I thought that was easy and the crisis was avoided. I thought I'd never do this again.

However, month after month, I found myself in the "Tiger Payday Loan office." I became such a regular; the ladies would address me when I walked in. They were my friends, or so I thought. "Hey Cedrick, what can we give you today?" Again, this bolstered my ego, and I thought I was a big man in their office. All the while, they were making a lot of money on my loans. But I didn't care because it was helping me make it through. **This is the trap.** I'll go back to the scripture I mentioned earlier. I was the slave to these lenders. I never missed a payment. They always offered me more than I needed, but I never took it. I knew exactly what I needed; that was all I would take.

THINKING MOMENT:

What would you have done in that situation? And how would you get yourself out of it?

_____
_____
_____

One Saturday morning, I was watching TV, and Charles J. Givens's promo came on. He asked, "Are you in a financial crisis and

EXTRAordinary Winning with Money

don't know what to do? Are you sick and tired of being broke?" I thought, yes, I am. I immediately wrote down the information on his upcoming seminar in Orlando. I put it on my calendar to attend. I was so excited to go to this event because I thought it would be a quick fix to get me out of this financial crisis. The day I went to the seminar, I quickly realized this would not be a quick fix, but it was a fix I needed. In that seminar, this guy taught us so much about money management that my head was spinning. I couldn't wait to get home to tell Tammie all about it. This new information inspired me.

He offered us an opportunity to purchase his Wealth Without Risk financial program. It would cost $200, but I didn't have the money. I told him I didn't have the money for it. He looked at me and said, "Cedrick, if you purchase this system and follow my steps, you will change your financial life forever." As soon as I got home, I told Tammie all about it, and I was sure this was something we needed to do. But we didn't have the money. So we started putting money away to save the $200.

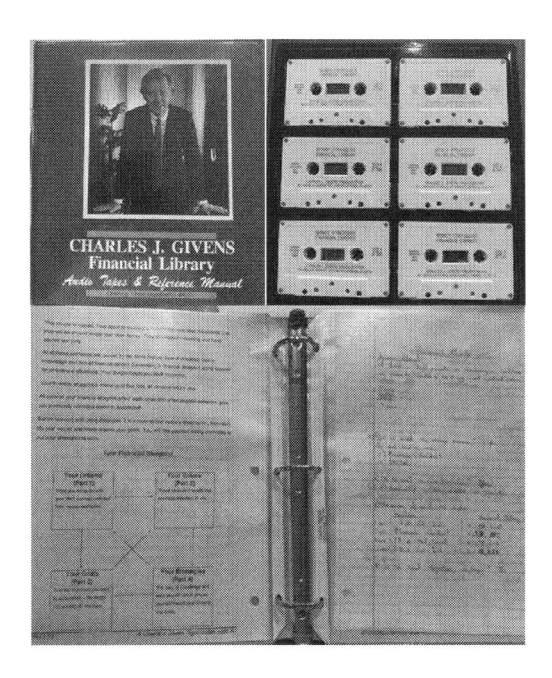

I want you to picture this situation. Back then, we lived in a ~$100,000 house and two paid-off cars, but we couldn't come up with $200 between us. But we had high credit scores. I thought this was pathetic. Don't you agree?

A few weeks later, I woke up and told Tammie, we can't continue to do this. It is not healthy. The information that Charles had given me was on my mind day and night; it all made sense. I found a local bankruptcy attorney to start that process, then got the $200 to buy the Wealth Without Risk program. Then we immediately went to work on changing our financial future. On the day the material arrived, we put a stake in the ground and said, "Never again," will we be in this situation. Then we set out to be intentional with our finances.

To help you understand how focused we were, I have included some documents we completed in late 1991 and early 1992. We had to take drastic steps to change our financial future. We were genuinely broke and did not want to stay that way.

On one document, you will see a checking account with zero balance, savings account with zero balance, an investment account with zero balance, a retirement account with zero balance, real estate account with zero balance. It appears we loved the number zero. I didn't include the house we were buying because, truly, the bank owned it.

We completed a Values List; I had never heard of that before. I needed to understand what was important to us. It does drive how you make decisions. Today, I teach clients about the power of a Values List.

We had to write down our financial goals. You will see we did not make a lot of money. But honestly, the money is not as important as what you do with what you make. I know some multiple six-figure people today who are broke. They spend

EXTRAordinary Winning with Money

more than they bring home. I hope this makes sense to you and will help you change your financial future. I've been there, and you don't have to; it's not fun.

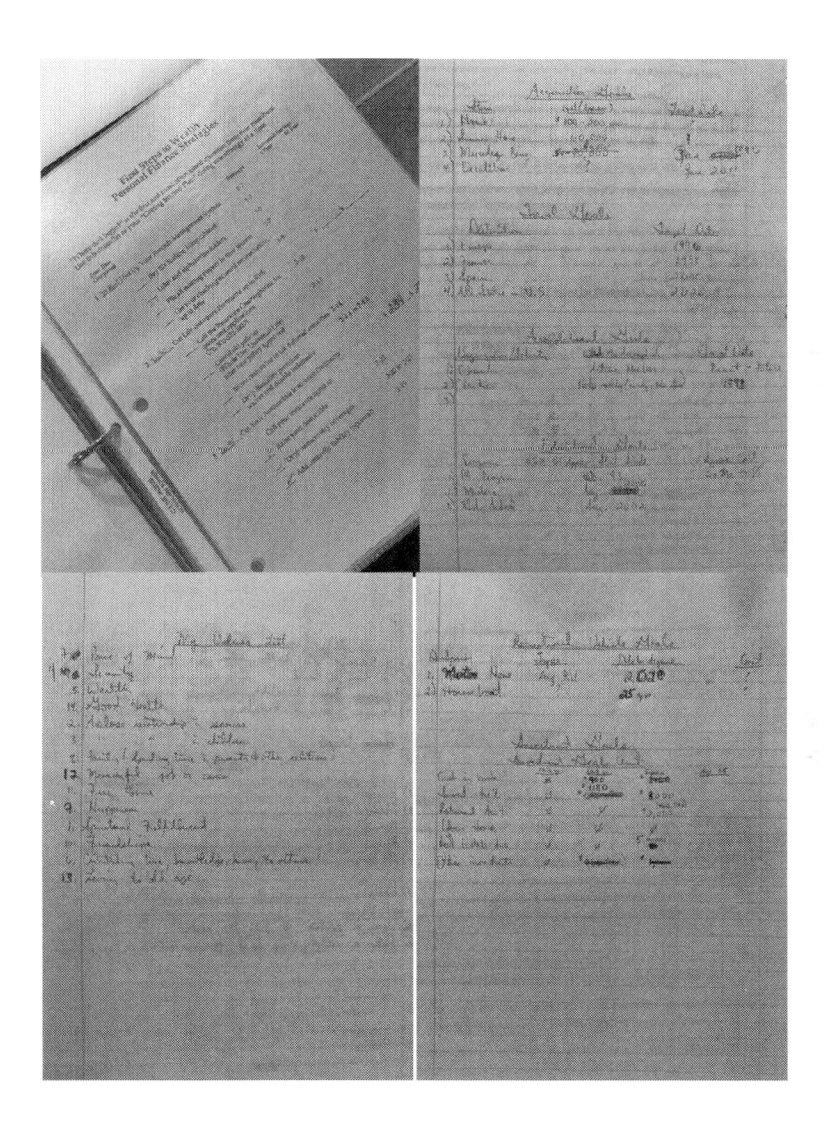

THINKING MOMENT:

The questions to ask yourself:

1. Are you tired of living paycheck to paycheck? _____
2. Are you tired of being broke? _____
3. Are you willing to change your spending habits?
4. Are you willing to say NO to going on vacation for a while? _____
5. Are you willing to say NO to buying a new car for a while? _____
6. Are you willing to tell your friends and family you can't spend for a while? _____

If you are unwilling to say NO to your old spending habits, you are not ready to take steps to change your financial future. Just know that's okay. Not everyone is ready to change yet. When you are sick and tired like we were, you can start the appropriate steps to take your life to the next level financially. Knowing you will have setbacks is essential, and that's okay. When you have a setback or emergency, you deal with it, then get back on the right track. Trust me; we had setbacks along the way.

If you said YES, now is the time to start. Don't wait until tomorrow, next week, or next month. Start while the fire is burning. It is easy to put it off, but more rewarding to start now. I recommend going to https://www.ramseysolutions.com/. The system works; you must change your habits. Embrace it all. Some people will say you are crazy. Some will say, don't do it. But that is probably, your broke friends saying it. Don't look at the car they drive; recall things they have said that didn't add up from a financial perspective.

THINKING MOMENT:

QUESTIONS TO ASK THE NAYSAYERS:

1. How much money do you have saved for retirement?
2. Are you financially sound to retire today?
3. Is your house paid off?
4. Do you have a fully funded emergency fund?

Too many people take financial advice from broke people. Don't listen to their advice if they can't satisfy the questions above. Just as you would not go to a dentist to repair your broken leg, you should not go to broke people to get solid financial advice.

We had to make difficult decisions. We had to give up doing things that some of our friends were doing. We would give vacations up, even driving to Lake Charles to visit family. We had to stop going out to eat. We had to stop buying extra things. Yes, we wanted to do those things, but if we wanted to go to another level financially, we had to give up all those things. In other words, to go up, we had to give up.

For you, think about this. Is it time for you to give up those Beyonce tickets? It may be not going to see Michelle Obama when she comes into town? Is it giving up buying the hair, and lashes, or jet-setting on that ski vacation? I know you may tell yourself I can get it at a discount, and I'm splitting the cost with a friend. But let me ask you this? What happens when you get on that trip, and you go out to eat, go shopping, and you see that outfit you must have? My point is you will always spend more than you think. What if you sacrificed for a short period? How much money could you save? How much better off will you be in the long run?

You can catch Michelle Obama on YouTube; it will be the same message. You can pull up Beyonce on iTunes; it will sound the same. You will get the same feeling. When you can pay cash for it, you will have a different feeling. Vegas will be there 3, 4, or 5 years from now. Wouldn't it be great to pay all cash for a vacation to Maui later vs. charging a cheap trip to Vegas today? I hope you get my point. I'm not judging; I've been there. I'm only sharing our experience on how to change your financial future.

I drive a Toyota today, but I could pay cash for Range Rover if I wanted to. I have no desire to do that. I would rather see that money grow. People only buy a new car every two or three to impress a person at the red light they will never see again. Think about it.

I also want you to know that bankruptcy is not the end of the world. You can come back from it. You can buy a house, reestablish credit, and have a significant financial future. You must also understand that it will not be an overnight process, it will take time just like when we were dealing with our bad financial decisions. I then had a conversation or revelation with God. During this conversation, he gave me a clear message, if you do the things I tell you to do, I will show you a life that you can't even imagine today.

Fast forward several years (I was 35) of hard work and economic transformation. We set new goals. I wanted to retire by 50, but we had to save $1 million. That was a message and my agreement with God. He said, if you save that amount and retire at 50, I will pour you out blessings bigger than you can imagine. That was a tall task for these two kids from Louisiana who had never had $1,000, $5,000, or $10,000 at once. However, I told Tammie we needed to set big goals, and if we were consistent and intentional, we could do it. She agreed with me but probably didn't believe that was possible.

I believed with all my might that we could do it. Again, I'm a dreamer and a believer. So we set out to do it.

We reached the goal two years early, so when I turned 50, I told Tammie I would be retiring. I couldn't work past 50 years old, or I would not abide by God's message. I'm sure she did not believe me because she knew how much I enjoyed my career. But I knew my last two years, the day I would announce my retirement.

In December 2017, I usually spent the month working on plans for the new year. However, this time, it would be different. I worked all month on what I would say to my team. I already knew what I would say to the organization because I was frustrated with organizational leadership and the lack of opportunity. However, I loved my team, and it would be hard to tell them. When you love your team, walking out on them is hard. I found it challenging to come up with the right message.

On January 2, 2018, it was the morning of our first team call of the year. I was nervous but excited. My decision was final, and I was ready to move on. I started our call just like I had done for 12 years. We discussed what worked well in the previous year and what we would do differently in the upcoming year. We had a good, healthy discussion. Just before we ended the call, I said these words,

"I have one additional change we are going to make this year. I will not make the journey with you all in 2018. I have decided to retire."

Here is the TEA

Someone asked, when? I said, "Today." "I will be here the rest of the week, but after that, I will be on vacation and come back to retire on February 8." I got off the call, cried a little, then called my director; that call was short. I said, "Good morning wanted to let you know I'm retiring. My last day will be February 8; let me know if you need anything. Thanks, and goodbye." I hung up the phone and never talked to him again. Now Abbott sends me monthly retirement checks.

How cool is that?

If we had not changed our spending habits, I probably would still be working that job even though I was frustrated. I would not have retired. I would not have had that option. A lot of God, much change in me, much prayer, and much change in financial habits gave me Freedom.

Winning with money gives you:

1. Freedom
2. Safety Net
3. Ability to help others

Everyone wants the **Freedom** to do the things they want to do when they want to do them. It gives you options, so you get to decide. If you have the money, you can quit the job you don't like. If you have money, you can move from that neighborhood you don't like. If you have money, you can pay cash for what you want. That is a generational mindset change.

Your **safety net** takes away worry. It could be an emergency fund that provides the funds you need to fix a broken car, take your child to the doctor, or repair a broken home AC unit.

Finally, **it lets you help others**. God does not give you great abundance just for yourself. He gives it to you to help others.

I'm not living with rose-colored glasses; I know not everyone will commit to changing spending and saving habits. I get it.

But if you do, you will change your life. Trust me, we were those people who didn't have a lot growing up, but we wanted something different for our kids. We slip every now & then and buy something we should not have bought; when that happens, we recognize it and try not to do it again. We take it one day and one step at a time. Don't stop. Don't quit. Stay focused on your financial goals, and it will come to pass.

Dave Ramsey at Ramsey Solutions created the 7 Baby Steps to Financial Freedom. (See the steps below). These steps are similar to the steps Charles J. Givens gave me many years before Dave Ramsey existed. I have added a Baby Step 8. If you follow this process, you will succeed at changing your financial future. When you peel back the onion, the lessons taken in these baby steps are the same lessons my grandfather was trying to give me years earlier.

Baby Step 1

$1,000 to Start an Emergency Fund (or $500 if you make less than $25,000 yearly).
An emergency fund is for those unexpected events in life you can't plan for. Whether there's a plumbing issue and everything but the kitchen sink is draining, or your brakes squeal at every stop sign, you can be ready! (We all know that Murphy will show up when least expected, your emergency fund covers you)

Baby Step 2

Pay off All Debt but the House
List all debts but the house in order. The smallest balance should be your number one priority. Don't worry about interest rates unless two debts have similar payoffs. If that's the case, list the higher interest rate debt first.

Baby Step 3

3 to 6 Months of Expenses in Savings
This step is all about building a full emergency fund. It's time to kick debt for good with 3-6 months of emergency savings. Sit down and calculate how much you need to live on for 3-6 months (for most, that's between $10,000 – 15,000) and start saving to protect yourself against life's bigger surprises, like job loss. You'll never be in debt again—no matter what comes your way.

Baby Step 4

Invest 15% of Household Income Into Retirement
Now it's time to get serious about retirement. With no payments and a full emergency fund, put 15% toward the retirement of your dreams. You have many options between your 401(k), Roth IRA, and Traditional IRA. Find the fit that is right for you. The money you used to attack debt can now help build your future.

Baby Step 5

College Funding for Children
College tuition and housing expenses continue to rise. Don't let college sneak up on you. Saving now will put you ahead of the game when your kids graduate from high school. Two innovative ways to save for your kids' college are a 529 college savings fund or an ESA (education savings account). These tax-advantaged savings vehicles let you save money for your kids' education expenses.

Baby Step 6
Pay Off Home Early
It takes the average family five to seven years to pay their home off early. Imagine life with no mortgage. Only one more debt stands in the way of Freedom from all debt! Apply all the extra money toward paying off your home. You are not only paying off your home early, but you'll also be saving tens of thousands of dollars in interest fees. Let me add when you have no mortgage. It is terrific. Your grass fills differently, and your doors open differently. It is a beautiful day when the bank has no interest in your home.

Baby Step 7
Build Wealth and Give
This is the last step and by far the most fun. It's time to live and give like no one else! Build wealth, become extremely generous, and leave an inheritance for future generations. Do you know what people with no debt and no payments can do? Anything they want! Now that's what we call leaving a legacy!

Baby Step 8
Buy Life Insurance & Create a Will
This is a bonus step but one of the most critical steps. There is one guarantee in life, we all have a reservation at the cemetery without the privilege of cancellation. Your family should be protected when you die. A simple term life insurance policy covers your family and final expenses. In addition, a Will lets you dictate how your possessions should be divided amongst family and friends. Provide your family with peace of mind when you are no longer here.

We followed those steps in the 90s to help us get here today. It allowed us to write a 7-figure personal check for our beach house without worrying about how to pay for it. FREEDOM is a remarkable thing. The number one thing money provides is FREEDOM. So when people tell me everything is not about money, I know they are saying they DON'T WANT FREEDOM.

No matter where you are financially, I want you to know you can change. I'll repeat that, you can change if you want to. If you desire a new financial future for your family, you must be willing to make some changes. Start with understanding your spending habits. For the next week, track every dollar you spend. Write it down. If you spend 0.15 on gum, write it down. If you spend $20 on a meal, write it down. Track it for one week so you get an assessment. Then do it for one month. You will be surprised at what you find out about your spending habits.

Once you have that information, then make some financial goals. How much money you would like to save in an emergency fund, in your retirement account, etc. Then you need to set up a budget that you are willing to stick with. If you need to get with a financial coach, then do that. It will be worth the effort. Remember the baby steps I mention in this chapter.

My commitment to God at 35

God would allow me to retire at 50 if I saved $1 million. We were so intentional with hitting the number that we reached 48, then $2 million by 50. And if I kept my commitment, he would bless me far beyond what I can see today. I kept my commitment, and his blessings continue to pour over my life.

A good man leaves an inheritance to his children's children, but the wealth of the sinner is stored up for the righteous.

Proverbs 13:22

"STOP looking at your calendar and START looking at your watch."

Ken Thornton

Chapter Five

EXTRAordinary Time Management

Improving your time management strategies will help increase your productivity. It is easier to reach your goals by improving your productivity. Increased productivity takes time. However, as you implement different strategies, you will discover which methods are effective and improve your personal and professional productivity.

This is the most crucial part of everything I will discuss in this book because time waits for no one. Once it is gone, it's gone forever.

Time management is the key to getting things done. It is easy to become sidetracked by unimportant tasks that don't help you reach your goals without proper time management.

STOP for 1 minute.
Do you chase everything?
Do you get a new purpose every few weeks?
Are you chasing but not sure what?
Are you never doing it?

STOP and do something. Work at it.
STOP & fail at it and keep trying in a new way.
STOP looking for something new all the time.
STOP. STOP. STOP. STOP.

IF it doesn't work in 2 weeks; try week 3.
IF it doesn't happen in 1 month; try month 2.
IF you didn't get a call back after one try, try 2.
IF they said no a 4th time, try a 5th time.

I didn't get here by abandoning the ship.
I got here by being persistent in 1 thing.
I got here by failing and retrying.
I got here by trying again, again, and again.

It's not microwave technology.
It's all in the oven. It's the slow cooker method.

John Maxwell states in his book *Intentional Living* that

"To accomplish our goals, live a life of true "intentionality." Be intentional at all times, in every way, and in all you do. This means focusing on making life better for others. That is the essence of intentionality, of living proactively."

The Benefits of "Intentional Living"
When you live intentionally, people notice. Being intentional:

1. **It gets people to ask, "What is significant in my life?"** Everyone should try to bring value to other people's lives.

2. **It motivates people to "take immediate action in areas of significance"** – Switching from "good intentions to intentional living" transforms thinking and lives. When an intentional person sees something wrong, they don't think, "Something must be done about that." Instead, they say, "I must do something about that." That's intentionality.

3. **It challenges people to "find creative ways to achieve**

significance" – Intentional living clarifies your perceptions and objectives. It helps you discover creative pathways for reaching your goals.

4. **It energizes people to work hard "to do significant acts"** – Professional development consultant Bob Moawad explains, "Most people don›t aim too high and miss. They aim too low and hit." Many people lack focus and have no direction for their lives. They muddle through, not sure where they're going or why. Intentional living changes that.

When I was younger, I wanted everything to happen right now. I still like to have everything right now; the difference is I have the patience to stay calm when it doesn't happen as fast as I want. I needed to develop my personal productivity rhythm.

Your personal productivity rhythm has a powerful effect on maximizing your daily workload and improving your overall time management. Your productivity rhythm will measure how, when, and where you are most productive; you can use these cycles to maximize your time.

Determining your peaks in levels of energy and focus will allow you to make better choices throughout your day and keep you on track. To effectively find your productivity rhythm, it is first essential to take the time to invest in yourself and your current habits.

Imagine you had a bank account that deposited $86,400 each morning. The account carries over no balance from day to day, allows you keep no cash balance, and every evening cancels whatever part of the amount you had failed to use during the day. What would you do? Draw out every dollar each day!

We all have such a bank. Its name is time. Every morning, it credits you with 86,400 seconds. Every night is written off as a loss, whatever time you have failed to use wisely. It carries over no balance from day to day. It allows no overdraft, so you can't borrow against yourself or use more time than you have. Each day, the account starts fresh. Each night, it destroys any unused time. If you fail to use the day's deposits, it's your loss, and you can't appeal to get it back.

There is never any borrowing time. You can't take a loan on your time or against someone else's. The time you have is the time you have, and that is that. Time management is yours to decide how you spend the time, just as with money, you decide how you spend the money. It is never the case of us not having enough time to do things, but the case of whether we want to do them and where they fall in our priorities. The next thing we must do is eliminate things.

Remove the Clutter

One of the most complex parts of organizing is eliminating the things that cause distractions and take up space. It can seem overwhelming when you find yourself among stacks and piles of stuff and items. But by taking it one step at a time and remembering to breathe, you can begin to de-clutter your life and start on the path to success.

People make things too complicated, usually because of **FEAR**.
Complication = Clutter
Clutter = Distraction
Distraction = Not getting started
Not getting started is because of **FEAR**.

Most people let fear drive their decisions both consciously and unconsciously. Here is how to determine if you are making a process too complicated. If you can't start immediately, you know it's too complicated. You should be able to start working on a goal or a dream immediately. If you can't, it's too complicated. You may ask, then, what do I do if it is too complicated? You start by asking three questions:

1. Why can't I start now?
2. What should I do to start now?
3. How can I start right now?

The answer to these three questions will provide the answers to simplify it and allow you start now. TRY it.

When I wanted to start CyFair Texans Basketball, I thought about who were the people who could help me with the dream, what did I need to do to get started, and why did I want to do it. Within two weeks of my initial thought, the business was operational. I immediately contacted the people I wanted to come along on the journey, and we were off and running. I lived in Chicago, IL, but the business would operate in Houston, TX. I could have given myself an excuse that distance would be an issue that would not allow me to start now, but I did not give an out.

You must understand I never played organized basketball; I wasn't a big-time athlete; heck, I wasn't even a small-time athlete. But I knew what my dream was, and I understood my value proposition. It was simple and easy to execute. First, I needed to recruit the coaches and teams I wanted; then, I needed to leverage my Adidas contacts to build the programs.

Just Do It

Ironically, I used the Nike slogan after just saying I was leveraging my Adidas contacts. But if you want to develop yourself, grow a business, and succeed in your career, you must JUST DO IT. I'll take it further and say you must develop a JUST DID IT mentality.

Sometimes we can feel overwhelmed about removing our clutter and make excuses about why it doesn't get done. We can claim we don't have the time or that there is too much to do at once. But as Nike says, we have to "Just Do It," and we must throw away our excuses and dive in. Make a plan on how you can get started, such as starting a business or finishing a degree, or going after a new job. Stick with your plan until the job is complete, and don't let the same excuses hinder your success.

Passion trumps obstacles and age. We need to reinforce that in our kids, Don't quit dreaming.
You are never too old.
You are never the wrong color.
You are never too disabled.
You are never the wrong political party.

It doesn't matter if you grew up in Goosport or River Oaks.
It doesn't matter if you went to Ralph Wilson Elem or TS Cooley.
Whether you graduated from Washington Marion HS or Barbe HS doesn't matter.
It doesn't matter if your parents are lower class, middle class, or have no class at all.

What matters is your mindset.
There is never an obstacle big enough to keep a person with Passion operating with a higher calling from winning.
YOU TOO CAN WIN, I DID, and many others did.
TODAY MATTERS.

Helpful tips:

- Make a calendar for when you will start
- Divide it into manageable steps
- List tasks
- Decide who can help you realize your dream

Know Your Energy

Next, you must accept that energy levels fluctuate throughout a day. It is highly beneficial to prioritize your tasks based on these energy levels. These patterns are connected to using brain power and thinking clearly. "Morning people" and "night owls" often describe one's most productive hours. Patterns of energy levels will differ for each individual based on various factors, including diet, sleep, or emotional stress. You can better schedule your daily tasks once you determine your peak performance times.

I'm most productive in the late-night hours. I seem to have extra energy in those late-night hours regarding my "thought energy level." New ideas come much better during this time. My vision becomes more precise and seems to flow better. Knowing that about myself helps me when I plan new things. I do it during the late-night hours. I've always been a high-energy (productive) person. I operate all the time as if I'm on a mission to accomplish things. That has been beneficial several times throughout my life.

It is essential to match the work of the highest priority to your peak performance times, including those tasks that require critical thinking or problem-solving. Likewise, you can assign your lesser complex tasks for the hours you know you will be less engaged or focused. Knowing your energy will let you set the stage for performing your daily tasks and seeking better results.

I was stationed at Patrick AFB, Fl, in the U.S. Air Force in 1989. Anyone in the military understands it operates in a high chain of command format. However, one day my supervisor called me into his office and said we want to talk with you about something. My mind immediately thought, what did I do wrong? To my surprise, the laboratory leadership wanted to discuss making me the Blood Bank and Shipping department supervisor. I was happy, excited, and surprised all at the same time.

They explained that they had been observing me and noticed how good I was at my job and that I took charge of situations. They stated it might raise eyebrows because several people outranked me, and they could be upset. They said that our Blood Bank had never been certified by the American Association of Blood Banks (AABB), which made standards for blood banks. They expressed that they wanted me to bring the blook bank up to meet their standards for certification.

This was not the first time I had been promoted above my peers. You will see other examples of this in the book. When your productivity is high, the rank will be a non-issue.

In the early 1990s, I worked at a hospital in Rockledge, Florida. I was a bench technologist in the clinical lab, and one day my supervisor asked to meet with me. She said you seem to be a person who is driven, productive, and likes Quality Control. Then she asked me if I would accept a position as the Quality Control/Quality Assurance person for the hospital lab and our clinic locations. This, again, was one opportunity that some people might get upset about. I wasn't the longest-tenured person on staff, but I had all the right skills for that job.

I accepted the position and began to transform how we managed and processed Quality Control in the lab. Our lab became one of the first laboratories in the U.S. that use Dr. James Westgard's Op Spec charts. I helped techs be more accountable for QC documentation. It upset the apple cart; however, it was important because we could kill someone if we put out a bad result.

It wasn't because I was the highest-ranked person, nor was it because I was the smartest person. I was far from that. I earned those positions because I maximized my energy at work, and I JUST DID IT daily. Not some days, not most days, not every other day, but every day.

Work-Life Balance

The most productive individuals are those who are well-balanced. This is the final step to better time management. Work-life balance includes prioritizing the demands in one's personal life at home and the workplace. This does not mean an equal balance of time between work and home but prioritizing what is important. Work time should be dedicated to tasks essential for your career, but home time should be dedicated to family or personal time.

I hear people say they don't have time to start their business, go on vacation or go to their children's activities because of work. Well, let me tell you a little secret, your employer will easily lay you off, cut your hours, and cut your pay. They will say, "It was a hard decision," but they still do it. If or when you get laid off, will it make you feel better if they said, "It was a hard decision?" Probably not. Folks, I understand that sometimes you must make sacrifices at work; however, what I want you to consider, at what cost?

One thing I did not want my teams to tell me was, "They could not make their children's event because of some meeting." We can make that meeting happen. Sure, there were a few things I missed during my career, but that was the exception, not the rule. I always prioritized making their events, even if I went back to the office to complete something or burned the midnight oil at home.

I remember my daughter's freshman year of high school; she made the varsity girls' basketball team. I was a sales rep covering the Texas Medical Center accounts. High-profile hospitals, demanding customers, and complex sale cycles. However, I was intentional about being at every game and tournament. If they were playing, I was in my seat. I remember one of her teammates asking her what I did for a living because I was always at the game. I was being intentional. Not once did I let work get in the way, not once did I miss any of my customer meetings, and not once did I miss a meeting with my manager.

My son played high school football, and every Friday night, I was in the stands. He played at the college level, and every Saturday, I was in the stands to watch him perform. It was not an option for us not to support our children's event.

When I was growing up, my mom could not make my Friday night performances, which was sometimes disappointing. I didn't get upset about it, but I was disappointed. I decided early in life I would be at my children's events. I remember looking in the stands at halftime when my mom was at the game to see her watch me. It made me happy that she could see me perform. I'm sure my kids felt that same way with us in the stands.

In the article, Parental Involvement in Your Child's Education: The Key to Student Success, Research Shows. Dec 14, 2022, by The Annie E. Casey Foundation:

"Decades of research have made one clear: parental involvement in education improves student attendance, social skills, and behavior. It also helps children adapt better to school.

In one instance, researchers looking at children's academic and social development across first, third, and fifth grades found that improvements in parental involvement are associated with fewer "problem behaviors" in students and improvements in social skills. Researchers also found that children with highly involved parents had "enhanced social functioning" and fewer behavior problems."

Be respectful of your time. Poor work-life balance often leads to working longer hours, increased responsibilities, and a greater chance of experiencing burnout. This work-life balance deal is about other people. It's about living an intentional life. Your children will never forget you sitting in the seat, cheering them on. They will always remember you hugging them after the event and saying you are proud of them. You can't put a price tag on that. If you are good at your job, good companies will recognize it and value it. Live a life of significance and value others.

Here is what I want you to take away from this chapter. I want you to value yourself, value others, and your time. How much is that worth to you?

Answer this question:

What can you do, starting today, to value your work-life balance more?

_____

_____

_____

_____

Practical Illustration

LaJuan is a guy that loves to go fishing. He goes as much as possible. He went out to fish for lobster one day and took a haul of 125 lobsters. He came home, prepped them, and put them in his freezers. LaJuan said, "I have enough lobster for an entire year."

He was so excited that his friend Kevin D. came over and he told Kevin about the big lobster catch. He asked him, would you like a couple? Kevin said yes, of course. That felt so good, he asked; I wonder who else would like some lobsters?

So, he started calling his classmates. And he said that he had a lobster trail to his house for the next three days. In fact, Kevin P. came over twice to get some. He felt so good he looked in the freezer after about four days and had only three lobsters left. Then he thought, wow, that was stupid. I had enough lobster for a year, and now I have only three left.

He said, I went away for a few days and came back. I walked into my garage, and there was this terrible smell. He wondered, what was that? He tracked the smell back to his freezer and realized the power had gone out on the freezer. He opened the door and looked; sure enough, those three lobsters had gone bad. He thought, OMG.

Then after a while, he started to feel good. He thought I'm sure glad I gave those other lobsters away. I added value to someone else. Otherwise, they could have all been lost. He said it changed the way I think. He felt the only lobsters I saved were the lobsters I gave away. The only lobsters of value were the ones I gave to other people. So, the point is, just add as much value to others as often as possible.

BONUS Time Management Tools

One Minute Rule

Everyone hates doing small, mundane tasks. They may seem unimportant, but over time, they will pile up, diminishing focus and wasting time. For example, if you do not look at your budget regularly, you will run out of money before the end of the month. This makes the simple task of budgeting much more difficult. Implementing the one-minute rule eliminates this problematic situation and protects your focus.

<u>According to the one-minute rule, if a task will take only one minute, complete it immediately.</u> If you look at your budget daily for one minute, it becomes an easy habit. Examples of tasks that follow the one-minute rule include: saving a document in a folder on your computer, putting clothes in the laundry hamper, and taking out the garbage. A minute will not put you behind schedule, and following the rule will save you time in the long run.

Five Minute Rule

Schedules only help people focus and manage time when done correctly. A common mistake that people make when creating schedules is to make them too strict. It is impossible to plan the day down to the minute. When creating a schedule, follow the five-minute rule.

<u>The five-minute rule is simple: allow at least five minutes between scheduled tasks.</u> This time is set aside so you can complete small tasks you have been avoiding or neglecting. The five minutes do more than provide time to complete small, seemingly unimportant projects. They also provide a buffer between scheduled activities, which will help keep you on schedule if a task runs longer than you expected.

*Leadership in influence.
Nothing more. Nothing less.*

John Maxwell

HALF TIME

So, you have made it halfway through the book, Million Dollar Beach House: My Journey to an EXTRAordinary Life.

You have learned about:

1. My background story and how we got started.
2. How motivation drives me.
3. What's required to be a daddy and not just a father?
4. How to win with money.
5. People notice when you produce it, and good things happen to you.

Hopefully, you have gained greater insight into how you CAN TOO, a better perspective on making massive changes in your life and drank a lot of TEA.

What are **two** things you will commit to in order to change your life?

1)_____
_____
_____
2)_____
_____
_____

Chapter Six

EXTRAordinary Leadership

No one had ever run a 1-minute mile in under 4 minutes until Roger Bannister did it in 1954, then six weeks later, someone else did it. Since then, the record has dropped to ~3:40s.

No team had ever played and won a Super Bowl in their home stadium until Tampa Bay did in 2021. Then one year later, the Los Angeles Rams do it again.

My first sales leader, Bill M., told me that when leaders show up, great things happen. I internalized that quote and committed it to memory. During my first year as a sales professional, I repeated that quote every time I visited a hospital for a meeting. I told myself I needed to show up as a leader for my customer, company, and myself. It is incredible what a leader's mindset will do for any person.

I have always been blessed to be surrounded by great leadership examples. But I have also been around some bad leaders. The bad ones stand out. I remember all the things I did not like about their lack of leadership.

I remember the ways they deflated the air in the room. I was in a meeting once with a bad leader; this person was trying to make me look bad in front of my team. She asked the team a question expecting them to say negative things about me. However, that didn't happen. During the conversation, I told the room to please say whatever was on their hearts.

I remember one sales rep speaking up, saying, "Can Cedrick change or do things differently? Yes. However, I have learned so much from him about being a sales pro. And I know he has our best interest in mind, so I'm good with his leadership." She wanted them to say something different. You may ask, how do you know that? Because she was so arrogant or ignorant that she admitted it later. But this chapter is not about those bad leaders we have all experienced but about EXTRAordinary leaders.
The first leader who impacted my life was my grandfather.

True leaders don't invest in buildings. Jesus never built a building. They invest in people. Why? Because success without a successor is a failure. So your legacy should not be in buildings, programs, or projects but in people. -Myles Munroe

As a child growing up in South Louisiana, I had the opportunity to observe outstanding leadership in action within my own family. My grandfather was a man of few words, but when he spoke, he spoke with authority. He was a man of influence. My brother, sisters, and I knew that when Pop said something, we had better listen.

Not that he would punish us or spank us because he never did that. It was that stoic look he would give us that encouraged us to do the right thing. Our obedience was directly tied to our respect for him. His presence exuded strength and fortitude. These traits enabled Pop to influence us and those around him.

Pop was a tall, dark, and handsome man. He carried much responsibility as the "Grand Leader" of his lodge. He was also a leader amongst his friends, a man of influence at work, and the definitive leader of our family. Whether he was called "Mr. Frank," "Mr. Washington," or "Pop," he was always spoken to with reverence, and I admired that. When I was at school, people knew him or knew of him.

When I was at church, people sought him for advice. And when I was in the neighborhood, people would say, "That's Frank Washington's grandson."

I can remember the many conversations we shared. He would say things like, "Save your money," "If you can't pay cash for it, you don't need it," and "You can bring a horse to water, but you can't make it drink."

I didn't understand everything he referenced as a child, but I listened. Pop died during my sophomore year of high school, but an ever-present memory from my freshman year supports the idea that great people live long past their Earthly lives.
During my freshman year, I was applying for scholarships. I received an invite from his lodge to go to one of their meetings. At least 10 of his friends were in the room when I arrived at the meeting. I didn't know what was about to occur, so I sat down, trying to figure out what would happen. One of the older men stood up and said, "Let me tell you about your grandfather." He then told me about my grandfather's significant role in creating a national education scholarship. The gentleman said something that left an indelible imprint on my heart. He said, "Your grandfather would always say, I didn't have the opportunity to get an education, but I want to ensure that future generations have an opportunity to get an education, and that is why we need to create a scholarship fund." In response to my grandfather's suggestion, the National Lodge created a scholarship named after my grandfather. THAT IS INFLUENCE.

Transformational leaders want to make a difference,
With people who make a difference,
Doing something that makes a difference,

At a time when it makes a difference. THAT'S INFLUENCE.

In my previous career, I was allowed to work on a team with a transformational leader. He was impactful and what most would call a "difference-maker."

I experienced his influence firsthand, and there is nothing better than working with a leader who understands the power of influence. A leader who understands the power of influence will often ask themselves, "Do I give people a reason to follow me?" If you are reading this book, you have also experienced the power of leaders who understood the value and magnitude of their influence.

The next EXTRAordinary leader is my role model, my friend, Mr. Joseph Nemmers. Joe is a man of influence. Joe is a leader amongst leaders who understands that leadership is influence. Joe is a retired Corporate President of a Fortune 500 company and he was in touch with people. He never let his title get in the way of showing value to the people.
One thing I remember so vividly about Joe's leadership style was his calm, cool, and collected demeanor.

I'm sure there were times he didn't like a situation or performance, but he never let it show.
I recall the time I first interacted with Joe in person. Joe was in Houston visiting the emergency sites during the Hurricane Katrina evacuation. Abbott was one of the major vendor sponsors supporting this effort.

I was taking this Abbott group into each location, and as we approached one security guard station in George R. Brown Convention Center, I said I don't know if they would let us through. Joe's comment changed my thinking forever.
He said, "Keep walking and walk like you own the building." We walked right through the security line with no one stopping us.

That was a mind-altering statement for me.
I have spoken to many people who know Joseph Nemmers, and we all agree that he is the ultimate leader.

Law of Buy-In - People buy into the leader, then the vision.

The next EXTRAordinary leader I was blessed with was Leo Serrano. Leo was a tough, no-nonsense Clinical Laboratory Director. He was the lab director for Wuesthoff Hospital in the late 1980s and early 1990s. I was a lab tech in USAF at the time but wanted a part-time job. Wuesthoff had a lab opening, so one afternoon, I drove to the hospital and completed an application. I had not received a phone call the next day, so I called the lab and asked to speak with Leo. He took my call, and I said, "I filled out an application but have not received a phone call about it." He asked, "When did you complete the application?" I replied, "Yesterday afternoon."

He laughed and said that was a great answer. He said, "I want to interview you just because you made the phone call so soon."

At that meeting, he said I'm hiring you because you called me. Great leaders make decisions fast and move on. Because Leo took a chance on me, I was bought into his leadership from day one.

Law of Timing - *When to lead is as important as what to do and where to go.*

Another EXTRAordinary leader I was surrounded by was my first sales manager, Bill Minix. Bill was a former military leader who led by example. He was sharp, detailed, and a great sales professional. I was living in Dallas and interviewing for an open position in Houston, where Bill was the sales leader. He called me one afternoon and said he was flying to Utah in a few days but had a short layover at DFW airport. He could interview me at that time. I said ok. Then he said, oh, you must meet me at 5 am at the airport. I thought for a second and said, sure, I will see you there.

Once hired, I dropped in the district sales office to show Bill a new customer contract I had closed, thinking he would be happy. At that time, we only had paper contracts. I walked into the district office and gave him the contract with a big smile. He looked it over, leaned back in his chair, and said we have a problem; we can't do this deal. I replied with a bewildered look; what do you mean? He explained that I needed to add more new business to make this deal worth it. As a new rep, I thought this dude was crazy (in my head). I said well, the customer expects us to ship them a new IMx analyzer and add those three new assays. He replied we are not going to do it. So, I thought I was calling his bluff, I said, "Well, you call the customer and tell her we are not going to do it." I had that young 30-year-old, cocky look on my face. He replied, "Ok, give me her number."

As I sat in his office, he called her. When the customer answered, he explained to her precisely what he told me. The customer replied, "Wait a minute, I have told my doctors we will bring those assays in-house; now you are telling me we can't?" He replied, "No, I'm not saying that." He then asked her if she could bring in one more assay, giving her a recommended assay. The customer replied, "Yes, we can add that assay."

My eyes got big because I knew how much that would add to the contract, but I also learned something at that moment. I learned to trust my leader because he knew what he was doing. I also learned never to be afraid to ask for more. He told me then, *"You don't get what you deserve; you get what you ask for."*

Law of Addition - Leaders add value by serving others.

Another EXTRAordinary leader I was surrounded by was Dan Stredler. Dan was my director when I worked in Global Marketing. I had a prior working relationship with him because we were in the same sales district. However, I was nervous about working for Dan because I didn't know his leadership style. To my surprise, he was a great leader to report to. Dan affected me on my first day in Global Marketing. He called me to his office and said, "We need to make a succession plan". I said, "Well, Dan, this is only my first day on the job. Why should we do that?" He said something that changed my thought process about leaders. He said, "If you don't create a succession plan now, you will never do it. It will also help me better understand how to help you. This will let me know what things are important to you and what you want to do next." Those words were like music to my ears. At that moment, I gained a better understanding of leadership thinking. Dan was a leader who truly cared about each of his team members.

We could tell that because he always asked how we were doing and if he could help us.

Law of Sacrifice - A leader must give up to go up.

The dream is free; however, once you start the leadership journey, you must pay. Dreaming of going to Hawaii is free. The journey to get there is a fee.

The Story: Martin Luther King Jr. eventually gave everything in leading the cause for equal rights. Even more significant than the sacrifice is that he was willing to do it. That was the strength of a leader.

The Lesson: Leaders must be willing to give something up and sacrifice if they will influence others. People expect that from great leaders.

I learned a lot from this group of leaders, but I want to be clear about what I learned from them. To understand who I am, understand that these people are high achievers.

One is my grandfather; one is a retired Corporate President of a Fortune 500 company at the time; another is a Clinical Laboratory Director, another is a Global Marketing Director and a Sales Manager.

High achiever-type positions, if you know what I mean.

These individuals demonstrated what outstanding leadership is. How great leaders perform, respond and engage others. I learned how to sell, how to market a product, how to make business forecasts, and how to be a great laboratorian, but most importantly, I learned how to value people.

I use three simple questions to determine if great leaders surround me.

1. Do they care for me?
2. Can I trust them?
3. Can they help me?

These are YES or NO questions. It is a straightforward process to make this determination. If great leaders do not surround you, I recommend getting new leaders. If they are, I recommend you listen to them, take their advice, and implement the recommended changes.

I could include many more leaders on this list, but you get the point. My leadership style and approach grew as I grew. As a young leader, my style was strict, no play, all business. I had the military leadership style, drive, drive, drive, and drive more.

One of my sales directors used to tell me to catch my people doing things right more than catching them doing things wrong. That did not resonate with me until one faithful day that changed everything.

My daughter was coaching college basketball, and one day I received a phone call. The person on the other end of the phone said, "Mr. LaFleur, this is Coach xxxx. I'm letting you know TK is in the hospital; she tried to commit suicide."

That news will rock you no matter what your job is, what you are doing, or what your title is. It rocked me. I wasn't expecting that.

I dropped everything, and we packed to get on the road. She was at a school that was a six-hour drive from Houston. We took off driving, and as we got about 40 minutes from our house, Tammie said, "I'm surprised you didn't think about taking a flight." I immediately pulled off the highway and looked up flights. The only thing on my mind was to get to my daughter, so processing getting a flight didn't even come to my consciousness. I just wanted to get there.

We found a flight leaving in two hours, so we diverted to Bush Airport. Once we arrived, we headed to the hospital to see her.

All I could think the entire time was, " What does she have to be upset about?" I knew the lifestyle we had provided her. I knew the advantages she had in life. I knew how well she was treated as a high-profile athlete, so I could not imagine her having issues.

Once we got my daughter back to Houston and with the doctors that could professionally help her. I asked her my burning question because I was at a loss. Her statement changed my perspective and gave me the total picture I needed.

She said, *"Dad, since I was seven, basketball has been my life; now that it is over, I feel lost. I feel like there is a whole inside that I can't fill."*

I replied, you were coaching basketball at the college level. She said, "That is not the same. Dad, you know how you say you don't know what to watch once the Olympics is over? And you fill this void in your schedule. That is how I feel about my entire life." Then I got it.

It's like a middle-aged guy who went into a cocktail lounge and went to the bartender and asked if he had anything to cure the hiccups.

And without saying a word, the bartender reached down in the bar, picked up a real wet bar rag, and smacked the guy across the face.

The guy was stunned and looked at him. He said that should do it. Do you have hiccups now? The man said no, but I never had hiccups; my wife was in the car. She has them.

Moral: You must get the total picture before you act or respond.

My leadership style changed from that moment on. The following Monday, I got on a phone call with my team for our typical update call. However, this time was different.

The minute I started the call, I told my team what I was dealing with, and these words came out, "I apologize for any mean word I said to you, and I will never treat another person like that as long as I live." My team responded tremendously well to my new leadership. From that day on, it was my goal to make them know, feel and understand that I cared about them more than I cared about their sales numbers. They automatically knew I cared about the number, but now they understood they matter personally.

So, now that you have unpacked this chapter and read about EXTRAordinary leaders, please take a minute to envision, imagine, and think about a leader who influenced your life.

Who is the leader(s)? _____
How did they **influence** you? _____

_____

_____

Why did it **Impact** you? _____

_____

_____

How did it **Empower** you? _____

_____

_____

You will probably smile, laugh, and even cry when you think about someone who influenced your personal life, career, or social life. EXTRAordinary leaders are special people who change everything.

The Story: Mother Theresa, although a frail little woman, became world famous as a leader among leaders focused on the poor, diseased, and youth. Although very outspoken, she was well respected due to her passion.

The Lesson: Mother Theresa had such a massive impact because of her influence. Her influence resulted from being a servant to others.

---

*You can't go to the
next level with part-time habits.
There is no such thing as giving 50%, 80%, 90%, or
even 99% effort and getting 100% achievement.
If you are partially in, you are 100% out.
Can you have success part-time? YES
Can you get to the next level part-time? NO*

Cedrick LaFleur

Chapter Seven

EXTRAordinary People

Purposeful Impact

EXTRAordinary people are all around us. They are a unique group of people who influence us with the words they use, their actions, and how they make us feel. Some fantastic people have blessed my life. The people I will share in this chapter probably have yet to learn how much they influenced me and some of my decisions.

From an early age, I enjoyed being around other people. I love the verbal stimulation. I enjoy learning how someone else thinks.

I grew up with my grandparents, and back then, children were supposed to sit in a room with grown folk and not say anything. I remember visiting my grandmother's friends with her, and I would sit and listen to them talk. I would only interrupt or say something if I were asked to. That is where my ability to listen comes from. As I entered my teen years, I started visiting my grandmother's friends alone to say hello. I found that I enjoyed listening to the "old folks."

I started noticing that I was learning new things and adding value to them by listening to them talk. Sometimes they told me the same stories two or three times, but I always acted like it was the first time I heard it. Sometimes I would not even go into their house; we would sit on the front porch.

One old lady whom we called Mrs. Queenie comes to mind. Every time I went to the liquor store (every day after school), I had to pass by her house while walking through the field. Wilson's Package Liquor store was the corner store around the corner from my house. We called it the liquor store. No, I wasn't going to buy liquor. I was a child. What are you thinking? LOL.

They sold all the snacks kids would eat, so I went there. Mrs. Queenie was always sitting on her porch when I passed by. I would stop and talk with her for five to ten minutes.

She was constantly spitting her tobacco juice out. We talked about whatever she wanted to talk about. Usually, it was something going on in the neighborhood. She would always say, you are a good kid, don't get mixed in with the wrong kids. I always responded, "No, ma'am, I won't."

Then I would continue to the store.

Once I got into the store, when Mrs. Wilson was there, we would also have a 5-10 minute conversation. She knew all the snacks I liked. Sometimes she would say, "My delivery guy brought your favorite today." I loved Oatmeal cakes with icing in the middle.

The brand she had tasted like homemade vs. the machine-made tasting ones they sell today. Mrs. Wilson knew all the TEA in the area. Again, we would talk about whatever was on her mind that day. Then I would say it is time for me to get home.

Another person that comes to mind is Mrs. Richard. Mrs. Richard was a schoolteacher who lived across the street from us. I would play with her daughter Vanessa.

Mrs. Richard was always asking if I had any homework and if I had completed it. I would always respond, Yes, ma'am, whether or not I had completed it. I wanted to play. But I would always make sure I did my homework before going to bed. There were many times Mrs. Richard bought things for my older sister and I if she had purchased something for her daughter. I enjoyed her taking us to see Holiday on Ice every year at the Lake Charles Civic Center. I enjoyed that show and looked forward to it coming to town each year. As I type this, I vividly remember some of the show's performances and smiling. If I could go to it right now, I would feel like a little kid again.

The final person that had an impact on me was also a neighbor, Mrs. Orelia Lavergne. Mrs. Orelia owned a hair salon. She welcomed the neighborhood kids to her house. She would say, "come on in baby." Once I got to high school, the "jerry curl" was in style and she was my stylist. Every six months I would go in for a new curl. If you needed to find someone to lift your spirit, Mrs. Orelia was the "go to" person because she always appeared to be happy.

Those are just four examples of EXTRAordinary people who helped shape me. I love the following quote, even though I don't know who said it,

"If you are a leader, you should always remember that everyone needs encouragement. And everyone who receives it – young or old, successful or less-than-successful, unknown or famous – is changed by it."

The people I mentioned did not have to take time for me, but they did because they wanted to add value. In life, it is not always about the people you encounter but the lessons they leave you with. These four ladies showed patience, effective communication, adding value to others, and the power of words. I was not related to them, so they did not have to add value. They were doing it out of the goodness of their heart.

People Before Business

The year was 1988; I was stationed at Shepherd AFB in Wichita Falls, Tx. I was a young airman, making little money. We moved into an apartment complex about 20 minutes from the base. We didn't have a car, and the bank wouldn't approve a car loan even though we had no bills. They said I needed a credit history. That was my first time applying to buy anything on credit. My grandparents didn't use credit, so I needed to determine what to expect or how it worked.

I would call a cab daily to get to and from the base.

For the first two weeks, the same guy (an old white guy) would show up in the morning and the afternoon. I would always pay him cash. Every day in the cab ride, we would have a good conversation; he was an old, retired military person. He would tell me about his time in the military and the bases he was stationed at. One day on a drive, he stated, "You can't afford to do this every day, right." I agreed but told him I had no other option.

So I would have to make it work.

He said, **"Here is what I will do for you."** He gave me one flat fee I would pay each pay period. It was a much better rate than if I would continue to pay daily. I agreed that I could make that work and pay him each payday.

So, for the rest of the year that I was there, he would show up at the same time in the morning, and I would call him in the afternoon. I paid him on time each pay period. Earlier, I mentioned that he was an old white guy; that was intentional.

During that time, race relations still needed improvement. In addition, consider that I was in Wichita Falls, Tx, where the city does not have a large black population. I am a young black man who he did not know. Our backgrounds could not be any farther apart. He did not have to offer me such a deal. He brought it up. He is an example of an EXTRAordinary leader who came into my life and blessed me. Yes, he was securing business, but he did not have to do that for me. When you develop relationships with people, barriers come down and get out of the way. A quote by Dr. Martin Luther King Jr. comes to mind when I think of this individual.

Life's most persistent and urgent question is, what are you doing for others? -Martin Luther King, Jr.

By 1989 we were shipped off to Barksdale AFB, LA. We enjoyed that base because Tammie's Godmother, Carolyn, and her husband, Julian Bell, were stationed there also. We got to spend a lot of time with them. Carolyn was a Captain in the Air Force, and Julian was a Senior Master Sargent.

They were well-adjusted in their careers, while Tammie and I were new to ours. Tammie was taking college classes at LA Tech.

Carolyn and Julian were so nice and accommodating to us. They let us stay with them until our apartment became available. In addition, they would always invite us over to eat with them and never ask us for anything. I'm sure they were thinking he is only an Airmen First Class, so he is not making a lot of money. They always encouraged us, whether they realized it or not. I looked up to them and where they were in life. I remember Carolyn had a Blue Toyota Cressida.

I liked the car's look and would dream of one day buying Tammie one of those. I would always remind Tammie, "Their paychecks can go much longer than ours, so don't you spend a lot of money when y'all go shopping." We didn't have bills other than rent, and I wanted to keep it that way.

Dr. Martin Luther King Jr said,
"Capitalism does not permit an even flow of economic resources. With this system, a small privileged few are rich beyond conscience, and almost all others are doomed to be poor at some level. That's the way the system works. And since we know that the system will not change the rules, we will have to change the system."

People make this world go around, and you must find those growth-minded individuals who will help improve your life. We all need champions in our life. Sometimes we feel we can do it all by ourselves, but that is not true. **You can't go through life all by yourself.**

Here are three questions you can ask yourself when trying to find those champions for your life.

1. Who can help me take my dream to the next level?
2. Who is willing to help me take my dream to the next level?
3. What specific skill(s) do they have that I need?
4. Why would they not help me?

Here are two Signs You Need New Friends (Champions)
1. Your current friends are stuck on celebrating what they did yesterday.
   - Yesterday = back in the day.
   - Yesterday = that one big thing they did years ago.
   - Yesterday = nothing new has come out of them.

2. You feel drained after talking with a friend consistently.
- If you feel drained, that person is taking value from you vs. adding value to you.
- Getting new friends going places and doing new things can be the pick-me-up you need.
  - Getting new progressive friends makes you grow.
  - Just because you change friends doesn't mean you drop the old one; it means you start limiting your exposure to that person (s).
- You don't need a drainer.
- You need a filler.

ASK YOURSELF: Are you a drainer or a filler?

This question is about you. You need to understand which one you are because we don't attract who we want people to be. We attract who we are; like attracts like.

The next EXTRAordinary person in my life is my sister Yvette. We both lived with my grandmother, and we were close. Since a young age, we seemed to mesh together even though we had two different personalities. She was outcoming and loved to go to parties, and I was the quiet one who enjoyed being home. Yvette was the free spirit who didn't mind talking back to our mom. I would never do that. I was too afraid of the consequences.

When we got to high school, my mom made me go to Friday night dances to watch her.

I wouldn't say I liked it, but she loved it. She would get on the dance floor to dance while I did my best to hold up the wall. I continuously checked the clock to see if it was time to go. It always felt like time stopped during those dances. I can remember looking at my watch, and it was 8 pm, then 30 minutes later (or so it felt), I looked at my watch, and it was only 8:10 pm. Our mom was coming at 10:00 pm.

I remember one dance at the ILA hall on Blake Street vividly. The ILA was only two blocks from our house, so Mom would arrive on time. When we exited the car at 6:30 pm, she said, "Be outside at 10:00pm." I kept watching the clock, and finally, seven hours later (or it seemed), it was 10:00pm. I was standing outside at 9:50 pm, ready to go.

But not Yvette; she stayed inside partying. Well, at 10:00 pm, when Mom showed up, she asked, "Where is Yvette?" I replied, "I told her it was time, but she kept dancing." **Here is the TEA.** My mom put her car in park and got out. I knew that was not going to be good. You must understand my mom was in her nightgown, slippers on, and rollers in her head. Remember, I said we lived only two blocks away, so all our friends were there.

Mom walked into the ILA Hall and went straight to the dance floor. I don't remember what song was on, but all I know is my mom started dancing in the middle of the floor. Soon the crowd spread and surrounded her, watching her dance. Of course, some teenagers were laughing. That was the fastest I ever saw Yvette get out of a building. Finally, she came out, and we went home. Let's say Yvette was never late again.

Yvette is the person that I've been closest with all my life.

Other people who have been EXTRAordinary People in my life are:

1. **Mike White** – He was the first person I learned how to run a 7-figure small business and what to do when you find the right person to help you realize your dream. He is also the

person who gave me my first Adidas contract. This dude is incredible at helping you think through a process.

2. **Paul Martinelli** – He is another entrepreneur from whom I learned how to run a 7-figure business and the mindset it will take to stay there. If you want someone to help you build a business, help you roll it out, and make a lot of money, this is the person you want.

3. **Christiana Richardson** – A young person whom I recently met who has the mindset to do great things. She is focused, driven, and determined. She reminded me of me when I was young; Very Intentional. I believed in her so much I hired her.

4. **Kimberly Dellafosse** – She's a person who is progressive and forward-thinking. I remember first meeting her at a Washington Marion HS alum meeting. I heard her speak and thought she was going places, and I have to introduce myself to her. That night I introduced myself, and we have been friends ever since. Her thought process was like mine.

5. **Aunt Ethel Mae** is my mom's sister and our oldest living relative. As a child, I always looked forward to her trips to Lake Charles from Sacramento, CA. She is a good storyteller. She is one of those people that I sit and listen to tell stories when I visit her. I'm sure I have heard them 100 times, but I love hearing her tell them. She laughs when telling them, which makes me laugh. I'm laughing as I type this, just thinking about her laughing.

6. **My other sister – Sheronda** is my youngest sister and another one who loves to party with friends and family. Although they never invite me. She will be the life of the party; you might as well accept it. Big heart. She is a little misguided sometimes, but she means well.

7. **My Bonus Sisters - Pam, Shun, and Earline** who I met in 2018-2019. They have accepted me into their lives, and I have embraced them as well. The first time we met was overwhelming, beautiful, and exciting. I love that we have come together and celebrated each other. My life has been blessed since we met. I have a whole new set of nieces and nephews, and I'm looking forward to continuing to develop our relationships. They genuinely have no idea how happy I am that we connected. **One interesting fact:** I was one of the hospital lab vendors for the same lab Pam and Shun worked in from 1999 – 2018(when I retired). But we had no idea of each other.

As you can see, my life has been filled with EXTRAordinary People who **Influenced, Impacted**, and **Empowered** me in so many ways. I am a better person because these people poured into my cup.

When fulfilled, you will reach a different level of satisfaction with your life. You will become more comfortable with who you are.

I ask these three questions regularly to decide if I need new people in my life:

1. Do I need someone new to help me?
2. How can they help me?
3. Why is that important now?

If I answer no to question #1, then I do nothing. However, if I answer yes to question #1, the next two questions will help me determine what skill that person should have.

Relationships are at the heart of what children need to learn, grow, and thrive. **Search Institute**

"Supportive relationships are critical 'mediums' of development. They provide an environment of reinforcement, good modeling, and constructive feedback for physical, intellectual, and social growth."

— **National Research Council.**

Chapter Eight

EXTRAordinary Kids

Whitney Houston said it best in her song, Greatest Love of All: I believe the children are our future. Teach them well and let them lead the way. Show them all the beauty they possess inside. Give them a sense of pride to make it easier...

My children are my world. They are the reason I do everything I do. From day one, when my daughter was born, my life changed. Then a few years later, when my son was born, I knew my mission to bring more children into the world was complete. **They are my blessing, and I am their blessing.**

I never knew I could love someone as much and as strongly as I love those two children. No matter what I'm doing, if they call me or ask me to do something, I do it. I believe part of that is a biproduct of me growing up without a father in my life. I mentioned in an earlier chapter I committed to myself that if I ever had children, I would be active in their life. I had so many dreams when I was a child of what I wanted my father to do, and he did none of them. It was so disappointing.

I used to dream about what it would be like if my dad showed up for me. Yes, I had my grandfather, but it was different. I could only imagine what it would be like. So, to satisfy my mind, I would imagine if it would happen. The dreams were so vivid back then.

Kem, Kelley, and Karla lived diagonally across the street from me. One year their dad brought them a go-kart, and he would bring it over for them to ride. I would watch them have so much fun riding it up and down Blake Street with their dad. Once they were done with it, I would sit on my front porch and envision if my dad did something like that. I would tell myself; he will do that one day. But that never happened.

Another one of my neighborhood friends was Jim and James; they were twins. Their dad, Mr. Butler, was tall, nice, and quiet. He would not say much to us when we were playing, but occasionally, he would interact with us. I always thought that was cool, that he was there every day. I would also imagine that type of existence. But I knew that would not happen. I did not want that either because I remember when I was younger, my dad used to hit my mom.

I mentioned in an earlier chapter I dreamed of my dad bringing McDonald's for my entire class. I used to walk home from school, thinking about that, but I knew that would not happen. Based on a lot of disappointment, I decided that I would be in my children's life. I never wanted them to call someone else dad. So, when I discovered that I would be a father, I already knew what I needed to do. There were four things:

1. Be present in their life.
2. Be active in their life.
3. Do whatever it took to raise them right.
4. Show them the way.

Nothing or no one was going to stop that.

My kids are just like other children; by that, I mean they are not perfect. They had issues when they were growing up, just like other children. They got in trouble just like other children did. They had chores just like other children. They didn't get everything they wanted, just like other children. Although some of my nieces had the misconception that they got everything they wanted. My children will tell you, they did not get everything they wanted.

Here is the TEA: I told them that if they got a scholarship, I would buy them a new car for college. Once TreKessa got her scholarship, she asked me for a Range Rover. I looked at her and said, "Are you crazy?" I don't drive a Range Rover; you won't be either. She got a new Honda Civic and loved it. You would think Patrick would learn from that experience. Yea, he didn't. He asked for a Jeep Wrangler with the hard top you can take out. Nope. I said, "Didn't your sister get a new Honda Civic, well, guess what you are getting a new Honda Civic too." He loved it.

However, where they separate themselves from the pack is in their ability to take action, dream big, and their mindset.
TreKessa, who likes to be called TK, is the firstborn. But I don't call her TK; I call her TreKessa, and when I'm upset, I call her TreKessa Lorraine. I could tell from the beginning she would be very independent and strong-willed. I got my first taste of

it when she was about a year old. She was a thumb sucker. Well, one day, I decided it was time for her to stop sucking her thumb, so I was going to take action.

I got up that day with no more thumb-sucking on my mind. Our normal routine was to dress her, feed her breakfast, then watch TV while I combed her hair. However, as I combed her hair this time, I put a sock on her hand. She tried to figure out what was wrong with her hand and how to get to that thumb. At some point, she cried, so I laid her down in her baby bed in another room. I figured she would cry herself to sleep while I watched TV. Five minutes passed. I was good with her crying; 20 minutes passed, and she was still crying but now a lot louder. I was telling myself she would fall asleep soon.

Now we are 40 minutes into it, and she is still crying, and I'm getting tired of hearing it. I closed her room door and said, I will ignore the noise. By the one-hour point, I had given up and walked to her room. She was standing in the bed, trying to see out of the room, looking for me. I took the sock off, and she immediately laid down, put the thumb in her mouth, and went to sleep for the next 1.5 hours. I learned that she would be determined to get her way.

Fast forward a few years; she was 4 or 5 years old. We were living in base housing at Patrick AFB, FL. It was a Saturday afternoon; she and her mom were at odds. I was sitting down watching TV. She said, "Daddy, I don't want Mommy here anymore. I want it to be just you and I." I asked her to repeat that. "I don't want Mommy here anymore. I want it to be just you and I." I said OKAY, come with me. I got up, walked to the kitchen and grabbed a paper bag from the cabinet. I gave her the bag and said let's go to your room and get a few things. She was following me as I walked down the hall towards her bedroom.

As I walked into her room, I told her to grab a few of "my" clothes (meaning her outfits, but since I bought them, they were mine). She put a couple of outfits in the bag. Then I instructed her to grab two of "my" toys. She searched, picked up the ones she liked most, and put them in the bag. Once she was done, I walked to the front door as she followed me. I opened the door, told her to go out, and as she walked out, I slammed the door shut behind her. So now she is on the outside, and Tammie and I are on the inside. She started crying and banging on the door while screaming Daddy. I just let her bang for about 2 minutes. Meanwhile, Tammie urged me to open the door and let her in.

I finally opened the door, and she rushed in. I told her that this house was for all of us and if she wanted to leave, she could. Then I walked back to the living room and had a conversation with her about respecting her mother and she should never say that again. I hugged her and told her to go apologize to her mother. She hugged her mom so tight; I thought Tammie couldn't breathe. And guess what, we never had that issue again, even when she became a teenager. You may wonder why I took that method of discipline. I wanted to make the point to her and felt a live demonstration would make my point very clear to her. Then I made her put all her stuff up and put the bag back in the kitchen.

When we lived on base, the children would ride their bikes to and from school. I worked the early shift at work, so I would be home when she got out of school. I would always stand in the driveway watching for her. She would come zooming around the corner with a big smile on her face saying, "Hey, Daddy." It always melted my heart when she said that. When I would come home, she would always run to the door when I arrived and welcome me with that big smile and say, "Hey Daddy."

Again, that would make me so happy. As I am typing this, I'm having flashbacks to that period, and it's bringing a big smile to my face. I'm sure some of that has to do with my desire to have these types of bonds when I was a child.

TK was an outdoors-playing kid. If I was outside, she wanted to be outside. If I was doing yard work, she wanted to do yard work. She was active and always wanted to work with her hands. I could tell she would be an athletic kid. Once we moved to Texas, she started playing team sports. That's when our lives changed. I coached her first basketball team, and later that year, she joined a new team called the Irvin Esteem coached by Rick Mels. Wow, that was a fun time in basketball. That team was loaded with all athletes, and they would beat every team they played, and I don't mean just barely, they were cleaning the gym floor with teams, until one day at a BCI tournament.

We faced this team out of Houston called Houston Hoops in the championship game. They were dominant. We could not get the ball pass half court for most of the game, their trap was on point. They had better athletes and dominated us. Who would know that a couple months later, I would get moved to

Houston. And she joined that team. She played for a couple more teams in the Houston during her early years. Then 8th grade she played with CyFair Texans. This was another team on another level. All high-level athletes who were starters on their respective school teams.

Because of this team's performance, we got a call to meet in Arizona to discuss a sponsorship agreement with Adidas. Coach Greg Cook, Coach Mike Ray and I flew to Phoenix to meet with them and walked away with a 3-year contract. Next, we had to meet with all the parents to discuss what they signed up for. I didn't want this to be just a regular meeting. We set up a meeting room at a local high school with a PowerPoint slide deck to make a sales pitch to the parents. The meeting went as we expected, and all parents were on board. Our first Adidas tournament was in Las Vegas, our kids were 8th and 9th grade, but we wanted to play in the 12th-grade division, so they put us there. There were 150 teams in the tournament, and we were running through those teams very easy. However, we never saw any of the Adidas officials at our game, nor did we see any college coaches.

We figured out that we were playing in offsite gyms away from where the coaches were. Once we got to the elite 8, we went looking for the Adidas guys. I told him, we have not seen you at any of our games, and we are beating all your teams. He replied, "I know, I have been hearing about it." He said, if you play this last game tonight, then you will be moved to the main floor, and it will wrap up the elite 8. I asked what happens if we don't play that game. He said we will forfeit but because it is double elimination, we will still be in. I said that then we won't play that game and rest up to play in the elite 8. He said, "Make sure y'all are ready because the teams you are going to play in Elite 8 are top teams in the country." I replied, "We are just looking for some competition." So, our kids rested up for the Elite 8.

The next day, we walk in the gym, and it is packed wall-to-wall college coaches. In fact, I held the door open for Pat Summit (Tennessee head coach) to walk in. Then I look and seen Jody Conrad (Texas head coach), Sylvia Hatchell (North Carolina head coach) and so on. It was raining head coaches. We lost the first game by 30 points. Then we lose the next two games by 40 points. Our girls were worn out. The Adidas rep and a couple of coaches told me it wasn't whether we won the game or not, it was good to see how these 14-year-olds represented themselves against this level of competition.

TK and all the members of the CyFair Texans team had very productive high school careers. All went on the play high-level Division I college basketball. TK played 5 years of professional basketball outside the U.S.

Children Can Adapt

At the end of her sophomore year of high school, we made a difficult decision. She finished the basketball season ranked #5 player in the country, the #2 player in scoring for the Houston area, and she was being looked at by a lot of colleges. This is usually not the time you move your child. However, my company offered me a position (I'll discuss this in chapter 9).

I accepted the position and had to tell her we were moving to Chicago. As you can imagine, she was not happy about it. Her high school coach was disappointed. It was a difficult decision but the right decision. To her, I was the worst dad in the world. I moved to Chicago before they came, so I thought I would rent a limousine to pick them up at the airport to ease the tension. That didn't work; she was crying as she walked off the plane. She cried in the limo ride home. For several days she didn't have much to say.

Once school started, it all changed. She met her new teammates then she started to expand her mind. If I fast-forward to the first day of school, the Baylor University coach was there. UConn sent a letter to her for the first day. A couple of local newspaper articles were written about #5 player in the country moving to Chicago. The first game of the season, a TV news camera crew followed her around like she was a star. They followed her during warm-ups, the huddle, and the game. She was finally adapting and accepting the change to Chicago. She realized that college coaches were still watching her, she could make new friends, and she would expand her network. I wanted her to thrive, and she did.

Here is the TEA: I emailed about ten high school coaches in the area we were going to live in to let them know we were moving there. I put newspaper articles about her in the email, and only one coach responded. Warren Township HS Coach John Stanczykiewicz responded. So, I set up a meeting with him, and the rest is history. Imagine the #5 player in the country is moving to your area and could come to your school.

This girl has given us some of the best moments of life and given us some dark days. To find out more about TK, you can get her book, Breaking the Silence – Basketball's Hidden Secrets on Amazon or connect with her at www.wintheballstops.com. Also follow her on IG or FB at @wintheballstops.

My #1 Son

Patrick and TreKessa are opposite in so many ways, yet they are alike in a lot of ways. Patrick was a quiet homebody growing up. But once he became an adult, you converted to an extravert. He is the ultimate networker.

On August 1992, as Tammie and I walked into Cape Canaveral Hospital to give birth, I was looking forward to seeing this little boy come into the world. We were ushered up to L&D, they started the process of the Caesarean birth, all of a sudden, they broke her water, and I could see this child's indentation on her stomach. They got him out, at first there was silence, then he cried. I looked over and said, "Yes." I was relieved that he was finally here. A couple of days later, Mom and son were on their way home. Every day I would hold him as I sat in my lazy boy chair, rock him and sing Amazing Grace to him as I watched TV.

Patrick was quiet but he would touch everything. You could not put anything down without him going mess with it. It was like he wanted everything. When he started learning to write, he got a little too happy with it. As he was watching the TV show Barney, in the living for about the 100th time, it came to his mind to draw. So, he proceeded to take a black Sharpie marker and draw a big circle on the carpet in the room. You may be thinking, what in the world? Well, if you are not thinking that, I was thinking it for you.

Always A Smile

Patrick was an easy-going child; he just kind of went with the flow. He always had a smile on his face. He would be outside playing and smiling. He would finish a sporting event, still had that smile on his face. I don't know where he picked that up, but he carried his smile everywhere. The only time I don't remember a smile was during a little league football game.

His team was playing in the championship game. The QB snapped the ball and handed it to Patrick to run. He tucked the ball and ran to the outside and as he turned the corner, the linebacker came around the corner and boom hit him. The hit was so hard, you heard it in the stands, the crowd stood up, and Patrick went down and stayed down. I'm sure his mother wanted to run on the field, but she didn't. I was standing on the sideline and yelled, "Get up, ain't nothing hurt but your pride." The other men started laughing while the coaches ran on the field to pick him up. It was a very hard hit. He came out of the game for a few plays, then went back in. He was just fine.

Boy, You Are Not From The Hood

Fast forward several years, we lived in suburbs north of Chicago, and Patrick was in 5th or 6th grade. He and his neighborhood friends were playing outside. Our subdivision of 30 homes was situated around Gages Lake on one side and some woods on another side. They were playing in the woods, and at some point, they came out and I was in the front yard. I looked at him, and he was dressed up like he was from the hood or in a gang. I asked Patrick, "What are you doing?" He said he was representing the "hood." All his friends were little white boys, and he was the only black kid in the group. I asked him, "Did you grow up in the hood? What do you know about being hood?" He could not answer that question. I told him to go into the house and change. Then I sat down with him to explain that we don't act like that. We don't represent something because someone said you should represent that.

I get it; children are playing; however, I don't want my kid representing some stereotype he knows nothing about. He wasn't born in the hood, he never lived in the hood, so why does he have to represent that stereotype? I told him, next time you tell them, someone else can represent "hood" if they would like, but he was not going to do that. The lesson I wanted him to learn was that representation is important. Don't represent something you are not, no matter who asks you to do it.

Patrick was also a natural athlete. It seemed whatever sport he played, he was good at it. He played MS and HS football, track and basketball. He took after his father. LOL. Talking about EXTRAordinary kid, he was a workaholic. He was always either working out in the front yard, back yard, or in the street. On weekends, he would say Dad, let's play catch. Yes, even in the hot Texas heat, we would go out in the street and run routes. Well, he would run those routes, I was throwing the ball to him. But he was a kid dedicated to his craft and always trying to improve. He was one of the starting wide receivers on his HS football team.

His hard work paid off because he was eventually offered a scholarship to play football at the college level. You don't have to be the biggest, fastest, strongest person on the field to play at the next level. Along with skill, you have to be willing to outwork everyone else.

EXTRAordinary Networker

Patrick is a relationship builder and a good networker. As I said earlier, when he became an adult, he shed his quiet introverted ways. He is definitely an extrovert now. After college, Patrick decided to stop playing football and pick up soccer. He started working on his skills, found a team, and played in tournaments. He was good at it. Then he started playing tennis, worked on his game, and now he plays tournaments around Houston. He is not just playing in tournaments; he has made it to finals in 4 tournaments. At the time of this book, he has not won the finals yet, but I know he will not quit.

UPDATE: As we finished editing the book, Patrick won his first singles tournament.

So, how does playing in these sports make him a good networker? He has continued to expand his network. He is always getting invited to events by these new people he meets. He has done a great job of professional networking within his organization and an even better job outside of his company.

Entrepreneurship

Patrick decided that he wanted to learn how to embroider, so he read about it, ordered an embroidery machine, got good at it, and officially started his business. He is a man of action like me. He has produced products for individuals, small businesses, and a major international company. I love the name of his business, and you should check him out for your embroidery needs. You can catch him at www.hashtagbillionaire.net. You see the name. That's EXTRAordinary.

I'm not trying to brag about my kids, but they have developed into awesome adults. A 19-year-old and 17-year-old kids who grew up poor have produced two high-level athletes. One made it to the professional level, and one at the college ranks. We raised two kids who also graduated from college with a bachelor's degree and one with a master's degree. We have been blessed to have two children who have succeeded in their corporate careers. That means they are not on our payroll. We have produced two successful entrepreneurs. Our life has not been perfect, nor without its challenges, but it has been an EXTRAordinary life for sure, and we truly have two EXTRAordinary children.

Here is the TEA: By the time this book prints, we should have our first grandchild, which we are so excited to have.

He will call me Pop and Tammie want him to call her Gigi.

**When you have the ability to
lead you should always lead**
*When you lead successfully, people will follow.
When people follow you, it is because you
influenced them.*
**When you influence people
you ae a leader**

Cedrick LaFleur

Chapter Nine
EXTRAordinary Career

Obstacles are necessary for success because in selling, as in all careers of importance, victory comes only after many struggles and countless defeats. - Og Mandino

Like most people, my career was not perfect; it had its share of challenges and obstacles, but I would do it the same way again. My career was rewarding, fun, adventurous, and worthwhile.

In this chapter, I will share some stories of victory and triumph. But I will also share some stories filled with obstacles, challenges and total disrespect. Some stories discuss great leadership examples, while others display poor leadership. There is always a lesson, whether the story is about wins or losses. And I hope you will find the lesson in each story. During some of my dark days, I tried to keep the "race card" out of it, although I felt race was a big part. However, once you pull the race card, you had better have definitive proof, or you could look bad. So, sit back, grab your cup of tea and let's go.

My first job was in the grocery business, but I had no plans to work in the grocery store forever. I greatly respect people who work in grocery stores, but I didn't want to stay there long. I had bigger dreams.

March 11, 1988, was the day I left for basic training in the United States Air Force. After basic, I would go to technical training school at Shepherd AFB, TX, to train as a Clinical Laboratory Technician. After completing all my training, I was assigned to Patrick AFB, Fl. I had never been to Florida, but we were looking forward to the move. We saw lots of pictures that the Air Force provided; back then, there was no Internet to get on, and there was no Google.

HERE IS A LITTLE TEA:

I was worried I might not pass basic training because, during one classroom discussion, the instructor asked what we wanted out of our military careers. With my young 21-year-old confidence, I raised my hand and said, "I wanted to be a military officer." The instructor, who was enlisted, asked me why I wanted to be an officer. I replied, "Because I see enlisted people as the ones who will do all the work and officers as the people who are in charge." (See why I mentioned my age). The instructor did not like that answer. So, he dove into me about how NCOs run the military. I didn't say anymore. But later, another instructor came up to me about my comment. I said I meant no disrespect, but he asked me why I wanted to be an officer, so I told him what I thought. That was my first lesson in understanding your audience before you speak. From that point in training, when I would pass by, that instructor would say, "There is the future officer because he doesn't want to do any work."

After arriving at Patrick AFB, we knew we would love it. The base is directly across the street from the Atlantic Ocean. Tammie, TreKessa, and I were like kids on Christmas day. There was no Ocean in Lake Charles, LA. We had only seen it in schoolbooks. It was fun. Then we discovered that we would live in base housing again across the street from the Ocean. We were living the good life, or so we thought. I believe that is when my thirst to live on the water was born, although I didn't like that I needed to wash my car every day due to all the salt. In the evening, you could see the salt haze in the air.

The Air Force allowed us to complete a "Dream List," your request for duty assignments. We could put up to 6 locations around the world. I went to the Personnel Office (CBPO) and put Patrick AFB for all six choices. I wanted them to know I didn't want to go anywhere else. We loved life.

Working in a military hospital is not just about working your shift and then going home. In the military, you have to be ready at all times to be called in for duty if the mission calls for it. So, I always had a bag packed in case we got recalled. When that happens, you must be in place within 1 hour and ready to go. Our mission was to provide medical support for Cape Canaveral Air Station, which included the Shuttle missions. Caring for soldiers and their family is a worthy and important mission.

With that said, we also took time to have fun. When I arrived at the base, our commanding officer was Colonel Thomas. He was a laid-back commanding officer. He made sure we had fun doing the job. We would always have medical group picnics and parties in the camping area on base. When you saw him in the hallway, he made it a point to speak and ask how your day was. I don't know how he remembered my name, but he did. The NCOs in charge of the laboratory were also great to work for. They made you feel comfortable, and being new airmen, my only experience was from basic training, and those instructors were not nice.

Sgt Boileau and Sgt Laughner were good friends who managed with a hands-off approach. I respected them because they were sharp and knew their stuff. You could go to them with any issue, and they would help you resolve it. Never did I have to worry about their rank. We had honest conversations even though they outranked me. They never threw it in your face. They knew their rank, and I also knew it, but we never had to discuss it.

In an earlier chapter, I discussed getting asked to be the Blood Bank Supervisor at Patrick AFB Hospital. Sgt Boileau and Sgt Laughner were the two people that discussed that opportunity with me. I wanted to make sure I didn't disappoint them. This was my first professional career job.

Six months after arriving at Patrick AFB, I enrolled in college to finish my degree. I enrolled in Warner Southern College and went to classes two nights per week. So, I would go to class every Tuesday and Thursday after working an entire 8–9-hour shift. I planned to finish my degree in the next two years, so I was focused and determined. As I completed each class, I would tell my mom I was closer to getting that degree we talked about. Then finally, I got the letter saying I was eligible to graduate, talking about an exciting time for me. I was excited about being a college graduate. I had two associates already, but that was not the same. This was completing my bachelor's degree. That was different for me. No one in my immediate family had graduated from college, so I would be the first.

SIDE NOTE:

This is where I want to discuss your responsibility to help others grow. Once I graduated, I started talking to some of the other soldiers in the lab and encouraged them to finish their degrees. Two followed my recommendation, enrolled and graduated with their degree. And if I'm correct, they each have gone on to get a master's degree. We should help other people advance as we advance. That is what **Influence, Impact, and Empower** are all about.

Once I graduated, the next step was to sit for the national certification exam. I registered for the exam and ordered study material, then every night, I would study at my breakfast table. I wanted to pass that examination to get a job in a civilian hospital lab eventually. So, on the exam day, I was nervous, but I kept telling myself that I would pass. I got to the site and saw a colleague in the room. About 15 people also sat for the exam. The proctor read all the rules, and we got started on a timed test. I started reading and selecting what I thought was the best answer. At first, I was zooming through each question, and then I got stuck. Then about 90 minutes into the 120-minute exam, I saw people get up and turn in their exams. I started getting nervous and asking myself, how are they done so fast, and I still have a long way to go? Then I see my colleague get up and leave. Now the self-imposed pressure is building. About 10 minutes before time was up, I had completed my exam. I looked around the room, and there were only 2 other people left. I thought, dang, I must have failed.

Back then, you would receive your results in the mail in about 3 weeks. I kept checking the mail, but nothing, then one day boom, the letter was here. I looked at the envelope several times before I opened it. I put it up to the light to see if I could see anything. I was looking for a BIG BOLD PASS OR FAIL. Finally, I got brave enough to open the envelope, then I slowly pulled the letter out and opened it. Then I quickly scanned the letter to see if I could see pass or fail instead of just reading the letter. Then I sat down and read the letter and in the first sentence it said Congratulations, so I knew I passed. I jumped up and screamed, then reread it to make sure I read it correctly. I wanted to make sure it didn't say, "Congratulations, you get to take it again." Another goal was met. I was flying high as a kite.

So by now, I had graduated from college, received my national certification as a Medical Laboratory Technologist, now named Medical Laboratory Scientist. So I was ready to tackle my new goal. I applied for Air Force Physician Assistant school. I felt I was on a roll, so I should keep going. First step, I needed to get several Air Force Physicians to write a letter of recommendation. I got the five doctors to write a letter. I also got the Chief Medical Officer and hospital commander to write letters for me. After putting my package together, someone reviewed it to ensure I met all the requirements. I knew it would be a long shot because they get several hundred applications yearly, but they only select the top thirty. About a month later, I received a non-select letter. So, I regrouped and prepared to reapply the following year. I had more letters of recommendation the following year, but again I received a non-select letter. I was down on myself but knew I would reapply. So this time, the Chief Medical Officer contacted his network to see what I could do differently. We made those changes and felt the third time would be the charm. But again, I received a non-select letter. Again, very disappointing, but I was prepared for it.

I had decided if I didn't get selected, I would get out of the Air Force. So, now I knew what my next steps needed to be. Here, I took matters into my own hands, skirting military protocol. I was determined to get out but knew that the current lab leadership team would not agree to let me out early. I was trying to get out 1 – 1.5 years early. This was a new set of leaders who I didn't necessarily agree with.

HERE IS THE TEA: I called Randolph AFB, which was the base where they controlled the laboratory staff levels. I discovered who the Colonel in command was and spoke with him directly to my surprise. I asked him if I wanted to get out early, what did I need to do and if he would approve it. He pulled up staff levels and said at this point, he would because the Air Force lab staff levels were good. This is out of the ordinary. Normally, you would go through your commanding officer to make these inquiries. He told me the steps I needed to take to get out, and he never said I had to get approval from my leadership team. He told me to go to base staff and apply; he would get the request and approve it. I did that the same day, and I received my approval within a month. I never said a word. I had several more months to serve, and I kept it quiet until I had two weeks left. I didn't even tell my close friends in the lab. Then I told the lab leadership, the Captain and senior NCO, I was leaving. They asked what I meant. I said, my service will be done in two weeks. They were surprised and asked did I have orders and when I received them. They thought I meant I had orders to transfer bases. I said, no, I'm getting out of the Air Force.

The NCO said, "Well, you don't decide that we decide that." I replied, "Colonel XXX has already approved it, and here are my final orders. They were in shock and immediately started making phone calls. Ultimately, they were told it was approved, legal, and final. I felt great.

I would miss my teammates, but I would not miss the senior NCO, my direct supervisor. This is an example of people not leaving organizations; they leave people. Again, what I did is not in standard military protocol, but sometimes you must take things into your own hands. In this case, I worked around protocol to get what I wanted accomplished legally—notice I said legally. I would never encourage anyone to do anything illegal. I did miss being in the Air Force, but my happiness was more important. The Air Force helped me grow, learn new things, and expand my network. It served its purpose in my life. My #1 priority was to finish my college education, and I had done that.

Before leaving the Air Force, I had secured a full-time job at a local hospital. Passing my laboratory certification exam helped make that possible; without it, I could not work in a civilian hospital lab. So, that certification gave me FREEDOM/Options. Remember, in Chapter 4, I talked about money giving you freedom. Same thing here; that national certification was currency.

After working at the civilian hospital for several years and rising to QA/QC Lab Manager, it was time to ask for a significant pay increase. I met with my direct supervisor to pitch the idea; she took it to the director, who then took it to the VP of HR. After about one month, the decision came back, no to a pay increase. I replied, "No problem, just know this is my six-month notification." The director asked what I meant; I said, "In six months, I will not be here." Then I called every vendor in which we used their equipment.

Here, I would leave because of pay, not because of people. I knew my value, and the hospital was unwilling to pay it. I was, again, leaving the organization, not the people. You must know your value, and if any organization is not willing to pay, you need one that is.

April 1, 1996, I was out traveling to an interview for a laboratory director position. When I returned home, Tammie told me I had received a call from Christy Shultz at Abbott Laboratories. I was excited but thought it might be an April Fool's joke. We spent the first few minutes confirming it was not a joke when I called Christy. Once she assured me of that, she told me they wanted to schedule a phone interview. The excitement started, and I envisioned myself working for a lab vendor. I ended up with interviews with two vendors.

About two weeks later, one vendor called to offer me a job, but the person said I would have to relocate. I responded, "You don't want me." She asked, why do you say that? I explained that they didn't want me if a multi-billion dollar company was unwilling to move me and I was not even going to make $100,000. I wasn't asking them to pay me $100,000, but I was asking this multi-billion dollar company to commit to paying for my moving expenses. Again, know your value. So, that call ended, and I wouldn't work for them.

A couple of days later, I again received a call from Abbott saying they wanted to fly me to Dallas for an in-person interview with a 6-panel team. My level of excitement jumped up. A couple of weeks later, I got on a plane to Dallas. I was prepared but nervous. I had made seven brag books, one for each interviewer and one for me to refer to. I had never heard of a brag book until a Deacon at my church, Ray Lea, helped me assemble one.

SIDE NOTE: A brag book is a set of documents that highlight all your personal and professional accomplishments. It is all about you. It's your personal branding statement.

I walked into the interview room and walked down the line giving each person one of these binders and talking about how they were impressed. One person said, "I have never been given one." I smiled and said, "I'm always prepared to be different." This made me win the interview before I answered any of their questions. The interview was going well until one person, Leslie M., asked me a question. She stated, "You are in grad school; how will you do that when this job may require you to work different shifts." I replied that grad school was optional, so if I needed to postpone it, I would do that.

Excellent answer, correct? At least, I thought so. The interview continued; then, she asked me a similar question again about grad school. I gave her the same reply. Then later, she asked me the same question a different way. I could feel my face changing, and inside, I was saying, didn't I answer that twice already. But I tried to hold it together, but I felt my face was showing my disapproval. We wrapped up the interview, and I left thinking I would be out because of that one question. I had dreams about that part of the interview for several days. I wondered how that question prevented me from getting that job.

Two weeks later, I received a call from HR offering me a job. He told me the salary and said we would pay for your move to Dallas. And wrapped up by saying someone will mail you a packet with all the information. Talking about being on cloud nine, I was. At that moment, I felt I had taken a chance on myself and won. I knew my value, and I wasn't willing to compromise. I never thought I wouldn't get what I wanted. This was my opportunity to impact my generational change goal.

SIDE NOTE: Leslie was the department director, and she was trying to see if I would change my answer. She and I spoke about it after I was hired.

"There is one quality which one must possess to win, and that is definiteness of purpose, the knowledge of what one wants, and a burning desire to possess it." - Napoleon Hill

My career with Abbott started great, we moved to Dallas, and I was thriving in our Technical Support Center. Two years later, I was promoted and moved to Houston, where I would serve as a field base technical specialist. Then one year later, I was promoted to sales. When I joined Abbott, I didn't want to be in sales until I saw what they did and how they did it; then, I realized I could be good at it. We were selling into the hospital lab, the department I worked in.

I WAS HOOKED ON THAT FEELING once I closed my first sales contract. When you close a deal as a salesperson, you get this euphoric feeling of success; it's like a natural high. I wanted to experience that again and again and again. I was so successful during my first 18 months in the territory I got promoted from a smaller territory outside of Houston to the Texas Medical Center, which is the prime territory. Our team was called the Houston Highrollers.

My performance continued to thrive once I moved to the new territory, although it required much more sophistication. The sales cycles in the Texas Medical Center were more complex, had bigger deals, and took longer to close. However, if you won a contract, it was a high-dollar win for a long time. I called it the stock market accounts. When you win, you win big, but when you lose, it is also significant. I spent a lot of time learning about each hospital, their challenges, and what they liked and didn't like in vendor equipment—and tried to add a lot of value. I made a considerable effort to make sure my clients understood that I was a former tech and not just another salesperson. I could become a strategic advisor for them, not just someone trying to sell Abbott products. It made a difference, and it showed in my sales performance. Within two years, I was offered a promotional job in Global Marketing. This was not just any promotion. I would have responsibility for Abbott Diagnostic's largest product line. That product had annual global sales of $1 billion. Think about this, the little black kid from North Lake Charles, who got married at 19, now in charge of a $1 billion product. I had to pinch myself. All those times I dreamed of being a successful businessman were coming true.

Abbott does not give the keys to the car to just anyone. You must be a high-performer type. And that person was me. I had a big responsibility, and I took it seriously. The lessons I learned about how to run a business, forecast, research, and marketing a product were endless. That was the most incredible two-year period of my professional life.

And two years later, I was offered another promotion, this time as a District Sales Manager. But I had a dilemma. I received one offer to move back to Houston and another offer to move to Minnesota. Well, that was easy; this southern boy had no plans of going to an even colder climate. In addition, the VP that offered me the position told me something I will never forget. He said, "If you want this opportunity, run after it with unbridled passion." I liked that statement and still use it today.

We enjoyed living in the Chicago area. However, that weather will test you. During our second year there, two things happen. We were going to Northwestern to watch their women's basketball game; as we got close to the street, we needed to turn on, the car started sliding on snow, and we ended up on the sidewalk. It was scary. And, during that second year there, the temperature went down to -21 degrees. No one should live in that type of weather, so that made my decision easy to take the Houston position.

We moved back to Houston, back to the district where I was a sales rep just two years before. Now I would be the Sales Leader of a $33 million business unit. Again, I reminded myself of the huge responsibility I had. This opportunity was different. One afternoon before moving, I reflected on where I grew up, what I wanted out of life, and now I got that opportunity. And I didn't want to screw that up. My children were watching, and I felt my family was watching.

Although I was excited about becoming the sales leader, there would be many challenges. The current leader was well-liked by the team, but team performance was an issue. The leader was not being fired; he was being promoted due to the company's reorganization. And now, the former rep is coming in to be the leader. I would not recommend anyone go through that, though.

I had been given guidance from the VP of Sales to fix the issues or get new people. It was clear what I needed to do. I took that charge seriously and did just that. Some people didn't understand it because everybody was friends. However, the company is not paying people to be here just to be friends. That's nice, but we were getting paid to grow a business. My job was to change the director of our sales numbers.

Here is the TEA: I had one rep tell me he had never worked for a black person before and had serious issues. He didn't think he could handle me telling him what to do. That comment caught me off guard and shocked me. I had not experienced that before, so it woke me up. Mind you, when I was his peer just two years before, he and I got along well. I helped train him when he was a new rep. As long as I wasn't telling him what to do, he was good with me.

The first thing I did was to call both HR and my director to ask how I should handle this. My director said, "You should not have to put up with that type of behavior." Eventually, he moved on to another job within the company. Something more substantial should have happened, but we moved forward. If I had told my white director I could not deal with a white person telling me what to do, I would have been fired. I'm sure of that.

You need to overcome the tug of people against you as you reach for high goals. - George S. Patton

Big Brother is Watching

Once we passed that, I was field traveling one day; my phone rang, and it was Global Security. I was surprised to find out what Global Security was. The person said we have a situation that you need to be aware of, and here are some recommendations for the next steps. Global Security is the department that tracks all electronic communication on the company's network. I learned at that moment, big Brother was genuinely watching. I was briefed on the activities going on via email with team members. It was serious, and they gave me recommendations. One individual attempted to have other sales reps provide false information to me. Trying to make me fail or look bad. But when you serve a God, he knows how to intervene. In all of my time at Abbott, I had never heard of Global Security; after this event, I never heard from them again. I call that a **God wink**.

Eventually, she resigned on the day I was going to terminate her. I was looking forward to terminating her because I was furious about her actions and her ethics. Especially since several years earlier, I was an advocate for her during her interview process. I prepped her for her interview. I figured she had been tipped off that she would be terminated, so she resigned. You see how that works.

Even though all of this was going on, I took it in stride and didn't make a big deal of it because I was concerned I would end up in the crosshairs because I was helping "friendly" people move on and move out. It was not lost on me that I was a black person in a white world. In reality, it was in the back of my mind. But I was not going to let individuals like this mess up my opportunity. I kept working on the plan, even though I looked like the bad guy. You must understand leaders must be willing to handle difficult situations, even if some people don't like it, and I was prepared for that.

Fast forward a few months after that person resigned, she made false allegations against me, including the stereotypical claims of sexual harassment. I learned of this after the case was over. My director called me one day and said, I'm in your city. I asked why are you here and why didn't I know you were coming? He explained that he was here to testify in a court case, then walked me through all the details of her allegation. It turns out this was a money grab from a large company. She could not give them any specific information to substantiate her claims. She had no direct statements I made to her. No action I took toward her. Absolutely nothing because I would not have hit on her if I was on my deathbed, and we were the last two people on earth.

The company realized it was a money grab, but it was easier to settle it and move on. I was upset no one let me know about the claims or the court case until it was over.

My director said the company does not believe any of it, so there was no need to involve you. But that didn't change that I couldn't clear my name. Everyone wants the ability to defend their name. It makes me very cautious today when I hear claims against someone until I hear all the facts. Let me say it doesn't mean there are no legitimate cases of sexual harassment out there. But this was not one of them. She was trying to get me terminated, but another **God wink** happened.

All this happened in my first couple of years as the new leader. After those years, we had the right team members to make things happen. We had a great rep in New Orleans always at the top of the stank rankings. We had a couple of new reps in the Houston area, a new specialist, a new rep in Memphis, and a new person in Alabama. Things were moving in the right direction. In 2-3 years, a new team and better outcomes.

Despite all the trouble, I enjoyed every bit of my new job. I took a hit to my reputation from a few people, but it didn't matter because I knew I was trying to get the team from the bottom of the stack rankings to a much better position. As you read earlier, I was a winner and always exceeded expectations, thus the promotions. I would do whatever it took to get our team back at the top of the stack rankings. As one senior leader told me, sometimes you must let go to go higher. What he was saying is you must let some people go to rise. You don't need a bunch of boat anchors. In other words, key doing the right stuff.

The Devil is Always Busy

After that initial road bump, things went well with multiple teams I led from 2006 – 2018. We had incredible wins. The company went through another transition in 2014, and I was given a new sales team and region. After the first year of transition, we had the #1 territory in the country. Not only did we outpace other districts in sales, but we also outpaced the entire U.S. by $1 million in profit. Let me explain, profit is the bottom line. It's like your net pay. Profit is what the company takes home. That is what you call EXTRAordinary sales performance.

Here is the TEA: Even with that performance, my director, who was a horrible leader, and her director figured out a way to exclude me and one of my reps from the President's Club. There was not a person in the organization who could believe it. I received many calls, texts, and emails apologizing and asking me what happened. I remember sitting down at a group dinner the day of the announcement, and my peers were watching to see how I would respond. I was quiet at dinner and just smiled. The next day, the leadership tried to justify their actions, but I didn't respond; I just smiled and walked out of the room. If I had responded negatively, they would have labeled me a whiner and not a team player and I refused to give in to that. My emotional intelligence was high enough to help me avoid emotional outbursts.

You can tell good leaders by how they respond during adversity. I just smiled and took it in stride. However, I was furious behind the scenes and let my senior leadership know. Early the next morning, I sent a detailed email with all the facts and data so they knew I understood what they did. I wanted them to know, I knew they had manipulated the rankings. They couldn't change the numbers (our sales performance), but they could manipulate the rankings. Not one person responded to my email, but I know they read it because I tracked who read it. Within one hour, all four senior leaders read the email, but no one gave me professional courtesy and responded. That's when you know, you know what you know. But I refused to make it racial and ultimately kept leading my team. Although, I believed race was a major part in their decision. It wasn't just against me, it was for someone else. I told my team they couldn't take away the bonus dollars they paid us, and they can't take away our pride, so keep grinding.

Again, this was one of those moments that could have derailed me from focusing on my goals, but I refused to let that happen. I was pissed, I was mad, I was frustrated, but I would not let them derail me. I was within six to seven of retirement eligibility, and this bump was not getting in my way. I could see that monthly payment in the distance.

Greatness is not measured by what a man or woman accomplishes but by the opposition he or she has overcome to reach his goals. - Dorothy Height

Difficult Decisions

Being a leader comes with much responsibility. You will have fun times helping people grow, expand and stretch themselves. But you will also have times when you must make some difficult decisions. There were two times I had to make a difficult decision to terminate an employee. With some exceptions, this is not something you should take lightly because it impacts that person, their ability to support their family, your team, and your customers.

My first case was when I hired a young man and moved him to Houston from Washington, DC. During the hiring process, we make sure reps understand they will go through a rigorous sales training process, and we take it seriously. I was excited to have a territory vacancy filled because it would free up my calendar to focus on the team's strategic direction.

The rep arrived in Houston, got settled then started our sales training. Every time we spoke, it appeared things were going well. Finally, it was time for the 6-month training to end, so he was off to Dallas for the final exam and graduation. It was early morning, I was sitting at my desk, and my phone rang. It was the VP of Sales calling me. I must add; this VP was an excellent, very laid-back dude. He was always smiling, and you could virtually see his smile through the phone. He would say things like, "Go sale some stuff." I couldn't imagine why he was calling me. I answered, and he said good morning; I also have our HR Director on the line. So now, I'm thinking, what's going on? He said we have a situation. He told me I would have to terminate my new sales rep because he failed the final exam twice. I immediately said, slow down. Can't we figure something out vs. firing him? I thought we spent a lot of money to move him, and he has only been here for six months.

His response and direction were clear. He said, "Well, Cedrick, you have a choice; either you read this script to him, or we will have someone read the script to you." Nothing else needed to be said. I replied, "Well, I am a company guy, so send me the script, and I will make it happen." I thought there was no sense in having two people get fired. So I called the rep and read the script to him. Then I hung up and called him back to ask, "What happened?" (I don't know if they were recording that call, so I didn't want to leave it to chance. If you know what I mean.) He admitted that he failed the final exam; they let him graduate but told him he would have to retake it the following morning. Back then, our graduation ceremonies were formal, followed by a big party. He had spent the night at the party instead of getting in his room and studying.

I liked the individual and thought he would make a great Abbott sales pro, but he made the decision. In addition, he was a black salesperson, and now I had to let him go. I was thinking, what was he thinking? It makes it hard for our race when we stumble like this. This is an example of you know the rules, but you want to make your own rules. We spend a lot of money in the onboarding process, compensate you well and train you well, but that comes with high expectations. So just like that, the territory I had just filled was vacant again.

Title Doesn't Make You a Good Person

April or May 2016 was the day I thought I would be fired. I was summoned to a call with the VP of Sales because he wanted to do what he did best. Tell people how bad they were when they didn't meet their monthly sales goals. He was the type of person who, if you gave him 100% of the goal, would say, why can't you get to 101%? You know that type. His personality was dull, and he could not relate to anyone. He was a detached leader. Have you ever worked for someone like that? We got on the call; I had prepared myself for the berating to start. He had spoken with a couple of my colleagues and scolded them, so I was prepared. He would say things like, "Your team is not good or not working hard enough or maybe it's just your leadership is not good." But today would be different. I usually just let it roll off, put my phone on mute and listen, but I couldn't take it anymore. I could feel my rage building up as he spoke. I stopped him, then exploded and defended my team; I gave him a lot of information to think about. I walked him through how we exceeded our Q1 goal, and that my forecast was that we would miss our April goal. So it's not like he didn't know already. However, I told him we would rebound in May and June. In addition, with the rebound, we would exceed our quarterly goal. I gave him specific details so he could understand I was not just making up numbers. I talked about each of my reps and how well they performed.

To his credit, he sat and listened. Then I discussed with him how deflating it was to be cheated out of the Presidents Club. I wrapped up by saying; I won't stand for berating anymore. I continued by saying, I know I'm a high performer, and my team is working hard, so I'm not hearing that anymore. He committed to looking into my accusations and would get back to me. But I knew he wouldn't get back to me; that's not in his DNA. He is the kind of leader that relishes catching you doing something wrong vs. praising you for doing something right.

He is not the one to give praise or appreciation. He looked into the numbers and had my director's director follow up with me to tell me I was correct. From that day forward, he never spoke to me in that manner again.

My point in telling these stories is not to discredit my former company because I loved working there, and I love even more being a retiree, but I'm telling these stories so you (the reader) see that not everything will always go your way. You will not always have great times. You will have some good leaders, some great leaders, but you will also have some bad leaders. That's a part of it. You need to have goals and act on them. That is where your focus needs to be. You will have those challenges that either make you weak or strengthen you. The challenges I experienced only gave me the strength to stay focused on my goals. One of my goals was to set myself up so I could retire at 50, and those challenges would not get in my way. I was making generational change for my family, and that mattered most. Those misguided people would not get in my way. I often prayed at my desk for strength before I would get on the phone with my upline. God will give you the strength, the power, the courage, and the ability to get through anything. And Lord knows, some days I needed it all. When operating on a higher plane, nothing or no one can stop you. Think of all the God's Wink you have had in your life during trying times. But also think about all the good times you had. I had great times at Abbott.

I knew I would miss working with many people. However, I committed to God at age 35 that I would retire at 50 years old. I mentioned the commitment in another chapter, but here it is again. God would allow me to retire at 50 if I saved $1 million. We were so intentional with hitting the number that we reached 48, then $2 million by 50. And if I kept my commitment, he would bless me far beyond what I can see today. I kept my commitment, and his blessings continue to pour over my life.

I was far down the road of making generational change for my family.

Here are examples of all the good things that took place during my time at Abbott.

- I could talk about our great times at the President Club.
- I could talk about our fun times at National Sales Meetings.
- I could go into detail about the company buying my Florida home from me when it didn't sell, so I would not have to worry about it.
- I could talk about my leader's compassion when my grandmother passed away.
- I could talk about the other amazing people who helped me when I needed it.
- I could talk about a time when our President submitted my name for the highest award an employee could win, the Chairman's Award, which I won. It has a fantastic dinner in Chicago, a nice plaque, and a whopping $10,000 check.
- I could talk more about all the promotions I received.
- I could talk about the VP who asked me to name any job I wanted, and he would make it happen. I passed on the opportunity.
- I could talk about the President helping one of my employees when his house was flooded.
- I could talk about all the community initiatives I participated in because of this company.
- I could talk more about how my reps showed me compassion when dealing with my daughter who tried to commit suicide.

Now is the time for me to put in another plug for you to go back and reread the chapter on EXTRAordinary money. I mentioned in that chapter the #1 thing money provides you is Freedom. I knew my level of freedom because I set myself up appropriately from a financial standpoint. I achieved generational change I had been working towards.

I worked with some incredible people. I learned a lot of lessons and grew as a leader. Some excellent leaders taught me a lot about being a great sales leader. I spoke about a couple of them in an earlier chapter. Abbott is a great company doing some incredible things with some incredible people.

As with any company, they still have some things to improve. I was there in 2022 for the 20th anniversary of Black Business Network. They have made some incredible strides in creating a more inclusive culture.

Knowledge is NOT power

Knowledge is POTENTIAL power It only becomes power when backed by a plan of action and then utilized

So please use the knowledge you have acquired; otherwise, it becomes stored information ONLY.

There is NO power in the storage of unused information.

Chapter Ten
EXTRAordinary Beach House

> *If you set goals and go after them with all the determination you can muster, your gifts will take you places that will amaze you.*
>
> ## Les Brown

In August 2005, we moved into our new house in Cypress, Texas. It was a beautiful 4500 sq ft. two-story 4-bedroom home in a great subdivision. We had an excellent media room and game room next to it. My office had a balcony, letting me enjoy the beautiful weather while working. We had excellent neighbors and an excellent lawn. It was a showplace home. Most people would make it their forever home, and I thought it might be our forever home. However, the first night we stayed there, I dreamed of a house with a 3rd story. The first time, I didn't think much of it. However, it was not a one-time dream.

Several times per month, I kept having this recurring dream of the house with a 3rd story. At the same time, I started envisioning living on the water. It became an obsession in all my thoughts. Part of this living on the water obsession probably was birthed on one of our many trips to Maui. Before Covid, we would go to Maui every 18-24 months. I couldn't get over wanting to live on the water.

I even convinced Tammie to look at properties on Maui. I knew that it was a long shot for her to agree to move, but for now, I was ok with at least looking.

For a couple of trips, I met with a realtor and looked at several properties. The dream was becoming real in my mind. I had vivid dreams about living on the water, and this 3-story house kept coming in. A few times, I would wake up thinking it was real. The 3rd floor had one big room with windows. I could see out the windows but not what else was in the room. I actually could see my neighbor's house out of the window. It was clear.

Fast forward a few years; it was now July 2018. We were one month away from leaving for Maui for 14 days. I was sitting in the living room watching TV.

A commercial stated there would be a land sale on August 4th. It caught my attention. I wrote the number down, looked at my calendar, and realized we would not be in town. So, I called the number to see if I could see the property before the land sale. The sales rep agreed, and the following weekend, we drove to Palacios, Texas. Before then, I had never heard of Palacios. I looked it up to see how far it was from Cypress.

The following Saturday, we headed out to meet with the sales rep. I did not intend to buy anything. I got Tammie to agree to "Let's go look." We arrived in the neighborhood and went to the model home. Honestly, I was not impressed with the model, but I was impressed with the subdivision. It was directly on the water, which was my dream.

The sales rep took us around the neighborhood; he eventually stopped on the lot we bought. We walked the lot, I went out to the water, and I thought, this is my dream. I said nothing; I just looked around, but I felt it. As we returned to the truck, the rep asked about my next steps. I replied, "We might as well buy this lot today." He was excited, but Tammie was in shock. She looked at me, and I said, "We are already out here; no point in going home and then driving back to purchase it." Then she said we would look in Maui again in a few weeks. But I asked her what are the chances she would agree to move to Maui.

She agreed that the chance would be about the same as a snowball chance of surviving the summer in Texas. We wrote a check that day, and the property was ours just like that.

A couple of weeks later, we went to Maui and still looked at properties, but we knew we had our lot. However, there was one house we looked at in Maui that was AMAZING. It was directly on the Pacific Ocean, the entire back wall of the house opened up, and it had a fantastic infinity pool. After looking at the house, we asked the agent for the sales price. I nearly fell to the floor when he told me the price. He said it is at a reduced price of $12,000,000.

I immediately told him the taxes on that house were outside our price range. But it was a lovely house to look at. We came away with some ideas for our future house.

Texas vs. Louisiana

Fast forward to September 2019, I drove past a vacant lot in Lake Charles directly on the Calcasieu River. Something captured my attention out of the corner of my eye, so I turned around.

It was a small sign about 12" off the ground that said For Sale by Owner. I immediately got out of my car and called the number. The owner answered and said he was coming to the property to cut the grass. Once he arrived, we walked down the property to the river. I instantly envisioned a lovely house on this 3-acre property.

The current owner already had a build pad on the property. I envisioned double driveways on either side of the property, lined with Palm trees headed toward the river. That turned into a common parking area followed by electronic security gates that opened up to the main driveway leading to the house. There would be a 2-3 story home with wrap around porch and deck facing the river.

A walkway went from the back deck down to the water, where there would be a pier.

After looking at the property, we stood at the back of the owner's truck and negotiated an all-cash deal. After agreeing to buy it, I called Tammie to tell her we could move back to Lake Charles. The phone was quiet, which I fi gured it would be. She has no plans to ever move back to Lake Charles. But she knew that was a dream of mine. So, now we had options, Texas or Louisiana.

Several months later, we asked the kids to visit Beachside with us. Once we arrived, I told them we would vote for which location to build. Everyone would get one vote, and the most votes win. I started to do the least votes win because I had a feeling about how this would go. The final vote was 3-1 for Texas. So, that was it; we would build on the Texas property.

Once that was decided, Tammie looked up floor plans online, and she is a C-style on DISC. For those who don't know, C-styles want a lot of data to review. I don't know how many floor plans she looked at, but the internet called me and asked if I could get her to stop. LOL.

Once she decided on a floor plan, I looked at it and said I was good with it. I'm a D-style on the DISC scale, and we operate in bullet points and bottom line oriented. I didn't need to see a lot of plans. Once we agreed on a floor plan, we provided that to the builder for review and approval. I won't even go into how the first plan was not approved because the house would not fit.

So that meant Tammie's C-style was back on the internet searching. Several plans later, she found "the one." It passed all the tests and the builder approval, so we were all set to build.

Selecting A Builder

There were several builder options in the Beachside area. However, I don't know if all of them want to work. We could only get two of them to return our phone call. When we got on the call with the first builder, he had reviewed our plans but tried to talk us out of building the house we wanted. He said, "You don't need an elevator; I don't think that will work." Right away, when we hung up, we both said he was out. Then we met with Lynn Construction; they came to the call with a plan to build our dream home. They satisfied most of our questions and agreed to sharpen the pencil on that price tag. Living on the water was coming at a premium. But we needed to get a good deal since we would pay cash for this house.

EXTRAordinary Beach House

Notice I'm giving the builder the final check,
and Tammie is taking the keys.

Finally, we agreed on terms; the build process started. I started making frequent trips to Beachside to watch the process. There are peaks and valleys with any custom build process; this was no different. Overall we are happy with the quality and workmanship of our new beach house.

As you may know, building a house is a big task and requires a lot of decision-making. What color floor do you want? Answer: Brown. What color brown do you want? There are 20 shades of brown. What color countertops do you want? Answer: White. There are 20 shades of white, plus another 20 with stripes or no stripes. Then you go through the same thing with every choice. We did not want to go through that, so we hired an interior designer to decide for us.

Interior Designer Selection

I put out a "recommendation request" on Facebook, and within a couple of hours, we had six recommendations. I started setting up interviews, and here is where small, minority business owners go wrong. They set up many roadblocks to speak with them. They try to call them processes, but they are barriers. You are a small business; why do you need Virtual Assistance for everything?

It's a novel idea but a waste of money for most small businesses in the beginning. Why should you spend 5-10% of your annual revenue on those things when you are just starting? It needs to make more financial sense. If they would look at their profit margin, they would likely find it's unhealthy.

We wanted to give this opportunity to a black-owned interior designer. We expected it would cost us between $70,000 - $100,000, and only a few black-owned interior designers ever get an opportunity at this level. So we thought let's be intentional with this decision. It almost ended before we got started. The assistant for the first company we contacted said the owner would not speak with us until we completed a screening with her assistant.

I said, that is nice, but I won't do that. I wanted to speak directly with the owner because I knew I would have to go through the same information twice. My D-style(DISC) would not allow that. She repeated that it was their process. I politely said, thank you for your time. We will not be using your service. Again, we are talking about $70,000 - $100,000 of revenue. I'm not talking to an assistant.

It didn't get much better with the following vendor we spoke with. The person wanted me to pay $25 for an application fee. Again, thank you for your time; I'm not doing that. I knew if they were worried about the $25 application fee, they would not be focused on a $100,000 strategic deal.
Small minds think about small things. Great minds think about big things.

Finally, I set up a meeting with three Designers. We interviewed a non-black-owned candidate to see if she met our needs. After all the interviews, we selected Nikki Klugh Design. We were impressed with her assessment process to understand our needs and preferences.

This was our first time hiring an interior designer, but I wished we had done this before. It made the building process less stressful since we did not have to make all those selection decisions. Before you hire an interior designer, understand it requires trust and a willingness to let go of control. We gave up control mostly, and on our big reveal day, we were pleasantly surprised at how well it all came out. Notice, I said we "mostly" gave up control. One of us needed a few reminders to let go. LOL

Growing up in Lake Charles as a kid, I dreamed of living this life, but I had no idea how it would play out. I DREAMED OF GETTING AWAY when I was locked in the closet at 5. When I was not getting the attention I wanted from my father, I started dreaming of another life. When my grandfather and I cut those "white people" yards, I dreamed of living in a house like those. When I entered the house my grandmother cleaned, I dreamed it was mine.

Those 19-year-old and 17-year-old kids have destroyed all the teenage pregnancy statistics. We have debunked the myth that kids from North Lake Charles will be a product of their environment. **Tammie and I are both college graduates. We have been married for 36 years to date and both of our children are college graduates. Our son has his master's degree. Generational wealth journey continues.**

We Could Not Control:

- Where we were born
- What family we were born into
- The color of our skin
- What others thought of us getting married so young.

We Could Control:

- Our actions going forward
- Own mindset
- Our dreams
- Our goals
- Our Decisions

Today, all those dreams have become my reality. We live in a big house, on the water, debt free. God has blessed us to be able to write a 7-figure personal check for this house. This is the generational change I dreamed about. We live a life where my kids call me daddy. Today, we're living our dream life.

As you have read, we made good and bad decisions and learned from them all. We would let anything or anyone hinder **OUR dream life**.

For anyone reading this book, my goal is that you learn how to set goals, take action, know your value, don't give up, don't listen to the naysayers and be willing to sacrifice.

The only difference between Ordinary and EXTRAordinary is EXTRA. The only difference between hot water and boiling water is 1 degree.

The only difference between your success & failure is MINDSET.

Successful and unsuccessful people do not vary significantly in their abilities. They vary in their desires to reach their potential.

Thank you for reading our story. Hopefully, I was able to **Influence, Impact, and Empower** you to go after your DREAMS.

That's all the TEA.

Two finals questions I would like you to answer:

1. What did you love?
2. What did you learn?

I was hoping you could send me an email: Cedrick.lafleur2@gmail.com with your response. I would love to hear from you.

EXTRAordinary Beach House

IT'S YOUR TURN NOW:

Now that you have read about my journey, it is your turn to start writing about your journey.

1. Use this section to start mapping out your plan.
2. If you want help discussing your action plan. Go to lafleurleadershipbooks.com to schedule a Million Dollar Action Call with me.

_____
_____
_____
_____
_____
_____
_____
_____
_____
_____
_____
_____

Million Dollar Beach House

Your Circumstance Doesn't Define You

A fatherless child has no excuses.

When I was growing up, I was told Horace LaFleur was my father. We shared the same birthday, February 23. He would always promise all kinds of things for my birthday. I would get excited and wait for that day we shared. Feb 23 would come and go, with nothing. I wouldn't hear from him for weeks after. Then he would say he forgot. As a child I didn't understand how he could forget since we shared the same birthday. From age 7 to 13, I was confused about that.

Now fast forward to my late 40s when I finally realized, accepted, and believed who my biological father was. His name is William Carter. So real my last name is Carter. Yep, Cedrick James Carter.

I knew him growing up until he was tragically killed in Houston when I was about 12. I only knew him as my older sister's father. He was always real nice to me; I didn't know why back then but it makes since now.

I remember when I was a grown man and Mr. LaFleur tried to give me fatherly advice, I wasn't having none of that. I probably was angry, but I got over it. I remember being angry at my mother for not telling me all this stuff before she left this earth. But I forgave her and figured she had her reasons. I remember forgiving family members who knew all of this but never said anything. I had to move on.

Young men, if your father (biological or not) doesn't show up daily for you, that is no excuse for you not to show up for your life, your child, or children. That is no excuse for you to not reach for the stars and become all you can be. That is no excuse for you to still live under the cloud of, "I'm fatherless."

- → You have your own life to live.
- → You have your own children to influence.
- → You have your own family to lead.
- → You have your own truth.
- → My grandfather stood in the gap for me.
- → My uncles stood in the gap for me.
- → My lord and savior stood in the gap.
- → My own self-worth stood in the gap.

Some of this makes me who I am today. A man who was fatherless but knew there had to be something better in life. A man who didn't let those parental mistakes that happen to him, INFLUENCE HIS ABILITY TO BE A GREAT FATHER. You don't have to let your circumstances define your outcome.

Author Bio

Cedrick LaFleur is a motivational and empowering Senior Executive with more than 30 years of success across the healthcare, sales, leadership, and sports industries. Cedrick has been married to Tammie for 36 years, they have 2 children, TreKessa (36 years old) and Patrick (31 years old).

Cedrick is the Chief Executive at LaFleur Leadership Institute, which focuses on building best-in-class leaders, keynote speaking and training.

Cedrick is an Executive Director with John Maxwell Team. He is also a Dave Ramsey certified Master Financial Coach.

Cedrick is the Chairman of the Executive Leadership Circle, which is a private organization where thought leaders discuss and address global topics. Finally, he serves as Founding Partner and President of Lake Charles Education Collaboration, Inc. a 501c3 Education Based Think Tank.

Cedrick recently retired as Regional Sales Manager, from Abbott Laboratories after serving for 22 years.

Thank You

Thank you for reading Million Dollar Beach House.

Leave Me A Review:
If you were able to learn and grow from this book, please take a moment to write a review as your words truly make a difference. Book reviews can be done on Amazon.com, or you can send me an e-mail at Cedrick.lafleur2@gmail.com with the subject line "Review."

Need Additional Leadership Mentoring or Coaching:

We exist to help build **best-in-class leaders** and to help you or your organization improve your market momentum. We exist to help your team deliver outstanding customer experiences. For team training, keynotes, workshops, or one-on-one coaching. Please visit www.lafleurleadershipinstitute.com Youth training: https://www.waveyouthleadership.com/

Want to Order in Bulk or Buy One of My Other Books?

Order books: https://www.lafleurleadershipbooks.com/

Made in the USA
Columbia, SC
13 March 2025